RETURNING
FROM
CAMINO

SECOND EDITION

Alexander John Shaia

QUADRATOS, LLC
Santa Fe, New Mexico, USA

Copy Editor
Lynda Helmer

Cover and Interior Art
Marc Heffner
www.caminoestrella.com

Interior Layout Second Edition
Eddie Cruz

Cover Photo of Author
Memoria+c Photography

*A mythological image that has to be explained
to the brain is not working.*

Joseph Campbell

There will be as many stories told of the cover image
as there are pilgrims who view it.

What is its story for you?

What do you see, feel, or remember?

is the registered U.S. trademark of
Quadratos, LLC.
Used by permission.

Other Books by Alexander John Shaia

Al Regreso Del Camino, Spanish Edition, Print &
Kindle, 2019

Rückkehr Vom Jakobsweg, German Edition, Print &
Kindle, 2019

Hazatérés A Caminóról, Hungarian Edition, Print, 2019

*Heart and Mind: The Four-Gospel Journey for Radical
Transformation, Second Edition, Print & Kindle, 2017*

Heart and Mind Community Guides, Second Edition,
2018

*The Hidden Power of the Gospels: Four Questions,
Four Paths, One Journey,* HarperOne, Print, 2010

*Beyond the Biography of Jesus: The Journey of Quadratos,
Vol. II, 2008*

*Beyond the Biography of Jesus: The Journey of Quadratos,
Vol. I, 2006*

may our return

be a gift

received

seen

given

in gratitude
for
Joseph Campbell
1904–1987

TABLE OF CONTENTS

Scallop Shell & Pilgrim Credencial
and my 1ˢᵗ Sello (Stamp)—1 October 2012

MY CAMINO STORY

With no forethought, I knew. A fellow doctoral student off-handedly mentioned something of an ancient pilgrimage route across Spain. Immediately, I knew I had to walk it. Decades flew by before I did.

It was the summer of 2012, and a series of projects and speaking engagements were suddenly cancelled. Very odd. Sixty empty days appeared on my calendar.

I fumed at the disruption, until a friend cut through my fog. "What might Spirit be providing you with this un-expected time?" she asked. As if a mouth was put to my ear, a clear, insistent voice said, "Walk the Camino!"

Six weeks later, with little physical prep, I set off from St. Jean Pied de Port. That early October day dawned brilliant, warm and blue. I was off, climbing the Pyrenees from the moment I stepped out of the Inn. Truth is, I crawled more than climbed.

One pilgrim who saw me, thought, "That guy will be home in a week." A month later, he confessed his doubt of me. He underestimated my perseverance. For years, this saying sat on my desk: "Given enough time, I can walk anywhere." The Camino proved this truth. Slow down? Yes. Crawl if need be? Yes. Stop? No.

By the time I set off over the Pyrenees, I had four de-cades of study and personal experience in leading rites of passage; and it was in those early days of crawling, that I first heard the whispers of this book.

I was on the cusp of age 60 and needed to do something to help my transition into a new decade. Could the Camino be that help? I would have no real answer until I tried.

As I walked, inner longings mixed with sheer joy and great serenity. Yet listening to other pilgrims and to my self, I became aware of missing elements in my inner preparation. Simply walking was not enough for me to have any confidence that I could make the desired changes once I was home again.

By the time I reached my turn-around place (Muxia), I was also hearing angst from fellow pilgrims. Most were just beginning to consider the return home, and its impact.

With lengthy daily walks behind me, I now had the time and energy to jot down notes about the walk, its gifts, challenges and my imagined experience in returning home.

Thinking back to before I left for Spain, everything I read or heard was about physical preparation: training schedules, packing lists, maps, and endless tips on how to choose footwear, lessen blisters or survive thunderous snoring. And there was a large network of support, both as I prepared to leave and while I walked.

Once I returned home, however, I discovered that my inner journey was just as arduous as the days of walking. It was a tumultuous period of joy, peace *and* bewildering confusion that lasted almost a year.

As an experienced passage guide, the inner work of returning was not a surprise to me. The surprise was the isolation and lack of support I experienced in doing the work. The wealth of support while walking had now disappeared. Nowhere could I find books, videos or even friends at hand who understood the challenges I was facing upon returning home.

Reflecting on my experience, and those of many other pilgrims whose stories I heard, I became convinced of the need for a guide that helps pilgrims prepare to return home.

Since that first journey, I now annually lead a small band of pilgrims on the Camino as an intentional rite of passage.

¡Ultreia y Suseia!

Your pilgrim brother,
Alexander John

1 May 2018, Muxia, Galicia, Spain

WAYS TO USE THIS GUIDE

You may be reading this before leaving for the Camino hoping to learn something that will make the readjustment to being back home easier. Or perhaps you recently returned and have discovered life at home a bit bewildering.

Then again, you may have been home for months and find yourself still wondering and sorting the Camino's impact.

Reading this book, even years *after* you've walked, can be of benefit, helping you integrate your experience. It is never too late to take up the work of homecoming.

This book is for you, wherever you are on the journey.

Reasons for walking the Camino are myriad. Regardless of your intent, this book will ably serve your inner—mental, emotional, and spiritual—preparation before you depart, as you walk, and especially returning home.

The book's chapters follow the journey, helping you build—step by step—toward a much easier homecoming and a rich integration of your walk into everyday life.

> *If you miss the moment,*
> *you miss your life.*
>
> John Daido Loori
> Zen roshi

As a guide, the book is structured to be read a chapter or two at a time. Reading in this way helps you stay in the here and now, especially as prepare to leave or during the time you walk.

If you are reading before you leave to walk, or as you are walking, I recommend that you do not read past where you are on the journey.

The one exception is Chapter XI, *A Classic Rite of Passage*. If you are considering making the Camino into a rite of passage, or are interested in knowing more about what is entailed in such a rite, please read this chapter before you walk.

"Monkey mind," a Buddhist concept, speaks of how intellectual knowledge actually interferes and hinders us from having a deep experience. We go to our heads, rather than immerse in the moment. My sincere wish is that you will empty your mind, be present in the moment and experience the peace that grows from simply being.

If your walk has ended and you read the whole book in one go, you will notice some material is repeated. This repetition is provided as a help for those who are reading just a chapter at a time.

The Camino is filled with a "muchness" that requires sorting. Likewise, these pages hold many suggestions. As you read, find the ideas that call to you, that make sense to you, and please *pass by the rest*.

Make this book an aid to *your* needs, and *your* home-coming. Just as each of us must make our own walk to someplace in Spain, each of us must also make our own way home again.

In this book, you will find the phrase "turn-around-place." Wherever it is that you end your walk westward—Santiago, Fisterra, Muxia or another place—that location is your turn-around-place.

Finally, though I speak exclusively of walking, I use that term to also include cycling and horseback, the other two forms of travel recognized for receiving a *Compostela* and/or *Certificate of Distance*, given by the Pilgrim Office in Santiago.

Chapter I, *Gifts and Challenges*, is an overview of a pilgrim's experience upon returning home.

Chapter II, *Before You Leave*, emphasizes a key counter-intuitive suggestion. The preparation for returning home best starts *soon after you make the decision to walk*.

Chapters III through VII describe one part of the journey. Each chapter may be read as a stand-alone.

Chapters VIII through X hold thoughts and suggestions about how to integrate your experience once you have arrived home.

Chapter XI, *A Classic Rite of Passage,* describes the elements, structure and benefit in a classic rite. It also includes a checklist for those wishing to make the Camino into a personal rite of passage.

At the back of this book you will find *The Story of My (Re)Discovery, The Journey of Quadratos Schema* showing the wheel of the four paths, and Joseph Campbell's schema of *The Hero/Heroine's Journey.*

Also you will find *Resources* with a list of books and films for further study, *About Alexander John, How to Connect,* and *Acknowledgements.*

I

GIFTS AND CHALLENGES

It is a strange thing to come home.
While yet on the journey,
you cannot at all realize
how strange it will be.

Selma Lagerlof
first woman to receive
the Nobel Prize for Literature, 1909

Coming home can, indeed, be quite strange. I thought returning from the Camino was the easy, joyous triumphant part. What I found was increased energy, wildly differing emotions, burning zeal, deep peace, an upsurge of agitation and a gnawing disquiet followed by months of wondering and sorting.

Considering how many pilgrims struggle with homecoming, it is surprising that there has been little available guidance on this subject. In preparation to leave for the Camino, you may—or may not,—have read many books, watched more than a few YouTube videos and listened to other pilgrims' counsel and stories; but you probably found no information that even suggested that you give forethought to your return home.

The joys of the Camino are real, deep and can last for years. Coming to the end of your walk, you may well have a profound sense of accomplishment, physical rejuvenation, rich reflections, deepened conversations, new international mates, a crystal-like clarity of heart and mind, a vital sense of being, and fresh purpose in living.

Equally, your return to dear friends and familiar settings can make homecoming an anticipated delight. No doubt, the Camino is often a mountain top experience in one's life. Many even review their life, describing it in terms of *before* and *after* their walk.

Please slowly re-read the two paragraphs above, especially if you are reading this book before walking. Try to internalize the potential feeling of joy and sense of accomplishment you may experience as you return home.

This book and its suggestions are about how to integrate that joy and accomplishment into your everyday life so that the Camino will be far more than a momentary spiritual pilgrimage or a fleeting glimpse of what your life at home could be.

Becoming aware of potentially hidden difficulties in returning from the Camino will benefit you in making the Camino an enduring mark on your life. These possible difficulties are real, affect many pilgrims, and might last for a very long time.

In fact, there seems to be some universal law that the depths and difficulties in homecoming are in some equal measure to the heights and rewards experienced while walking.

First-time pilgrims and veterans alike have struggled with how to come home from walking the Camino because we largely live in a culture focused on attaining a goal or arriving at a destination.

On the Camino that goal is almost exclusively described as "getting to Santiago." Even among pilgrims who have walked multiple times, some are still at a loss for how to integrate the experience because their goal was more getting to a destination, rather than an inner journey lasting far longer than arriving back home.

Homecoming is challenging enough but can be compounded by the fact that trying to talk about the Camino with those who have not *had* a similar experience often isn't helpful.

Those who have not walked the Camino, nor had other forms of a deeply transformative experience, will find the Camino's power and impact difficult to appreciate. This can leave the pilgrim-at-home feeling even more isolated.

Most pilgrims (not all) that I have met describe some manner of difficulties, including disorientation, upon their return. Being aware that disorientation is possible is a powerful aid in easing the difficulty. Know too—you are not alone in facing the trials of readjustment to life post-walking.

Once home, our lessened physical activity can result in uncomfortable muscular adjustments, duller sensory experiences, decreased endorphins, weaker mind-body connection and a level of caloric intake that is too high for the decreased amount of physical exercise, resulting in possible weight gain as well as loss of muscle tone.

While walking, life is pared down and simplified. We carry everything in a pack and shop only for light-weight essentials. Returning to our day to day lives, we may easily become overwhelmed. At home, the number of items to choose from in a store can be mind-numbing, overloading our senses and even making our stomachs turn.

Noticing our accumulation of material objects around where we live might leave us feeling closed-in and claustrophobic. As we walk, the daily to-do list is minimal. Once home, tasks flood in, and our equanimity may easily be swept away.

Being in a large anonymous crowd after the intimacy of a pilgrim community can bring grief or free-floating anxiety. Before the Camino, we might have taken the *muchness* of modern life for granted. After walking, the muchness of modern life can seem *too* much, leading us to withdraw, feel acute loneliness or even experience depression.

We miss the depth of connection, the sense of recognition, and the mutual care we experienced with other pilgrims. Returning home, even conversations with old friends and family can now seem lifeless and superficial.

As we walk, we may find ourselves living a new outlook on life; one that seems clear, significant and self-evident. Among the many positive results, the Camino often awakens our desire to live more simply and with greater authenticity.

However, upon our return home that new perspective may not be supported by our family and closest friends.

Returning to life at home, we begin to question ourselves. We may doubt our own truths and wonder how or if it is even possible to bring the Camino into everyday life.

If we have begun to grow or change in either subtle or dramatic ways while walking the Camino, our arrival back home will by necessity be met with a sense of uncertainty, tests, and some manner of chaos.

Do not be discouraged! Each of the challenges of homecoming is connected in equal measure to the abiding joy found through making this pilgrimage.

Homecoming is not post-Camino!

Homecoming is the final, critical part of the journey where we gradually learn how to put into effect the changes that were awakened in us as we walked.

More than easing the difficulties of returning home, utilizing the suggestions found within these pages will help our walk be the rich Camino experience we want, with its effects likely to endure for many, many years.

II

BEFORE YOU LEAVE

Nothing natural or interesting goes in a straight line. As a matter of fact, it is the quickest way to the wrong place.

And don't pretend you know where you are going. Because if you know where you are going, that means you've already been there, and you are going to end up exactly where you came from.

Naomi Newman
from the play Snake Talk:
Urgent Messages from the Mother

Taking time to consider your return from the Camino *before* you leave may seem one thing you can easily leave off your list. Counter-intuitive as it may be, every moment spent considering the time after your boots come off will benefit you both during the walk and especially upon your return.

Understanding the need for a bit of preparation for your return is likely hard. I am asking you to trust my recommendation to put these five pieces in place before you leave:

- Choose a companion/mentor and ask for their presence with you when you return, to hear your story and deepening reflections
- Choose a mental attitude of staying in the present moment
- Learn to value uncertainty and some anxiety as requisite inner companions
- Ponder what needs to change in your life
- Make initial (tentative) plans for the time immediately after you end walking as well as when you arrive home

Everything you do before you leave, as you walk, and at your turn-around-place will begin to bear rich fruit when you return home.

I Am Walking Because...

Reflect on the reason(s) you are walking the Camino. Make a list as long as you wish. You may be dealing with health issues or feel in your prime. You may have recently lost a job or are about to begin a new one. You may have experienced the end of a marriage, or you may be a newlywed. Then again, maybe that spark in life has dimmed, or you are seeking a renewed sense of meaning and purpose.

Before you walk, it is *not* important to know the reasons, or be able to clearly define what you want to change. Clarity usually arrives as you walk or when you come to the end of your walking. At the beginning, all you need to know is that you are seeking something.

Yes, some begin the Camino on a lark, as a walking holiday or an adventure trek. But these accidental pilgrims often find the Camino impacting them more than they expected.

There are many reasons for walking the Camino: emotional, intellectual, physical, religious, spiritual, and accidental. All of them are valid, and the ideas here will be of benefit regardless of the reasons you are walking.

Four Stages of the Camino

Regardless of your reason for walking, you may see the Camino as having four stages: 1. leaving for the Camino; 2. walking; 3. arriving at a particular place; 4. returning home. Describing a great journey in four parts is as ancient as human storytelling.

Joseph Campbell, one of the world's pre-eminent mythologists, described the sequence in any human quest—the hero or heroine's journey—in four stages:

- Hearing the Summons & Crossing a Threshold
- Enduring Trials and Obstacles
- Receiving the Boon or Gift
- Crossing a Threshold & Returning Home with Larger Responsibility

For more on Joseph Campbell and his schema of *The Hero-Heroine's Journey*, see page 125ff.

Building on Campbell's work, I see the story of a quest as the journey of growth and transformation for everyone. I name this *The Journey of Quadratos*, which is comprised of four paths.

- *1ˢᵗ Path, Facing Change:* Hearing the call, deciding to go, and setting out.

- *2ⁿᵈ Path, Moving Through Trials and Obstacles:* Meeting physical, emotional, and spiritual obstacles as you walk.

- *3ʳᵈ Path, Receiving Joy and Experiencing Oneness:* Sense of deep peace, joy and/or gift-edness that arrive usually by surprise, somewhere while walking.

- *4ᵗʰ Path, Maturing in Service:* Returning home to build skills in sharing your gift.

For more on *The Journey of Quadratos* and its schema, see page 119ff.

If your intent is to walk because something in your life needs further reflection and change, then your Camino by definition is a journey for personal growth and transformation.

Viewing your walk through the paradigm of the four stages can provide an internal map for your Camino as well as with the to-be-expected bewilderment upon homecoming.

Adding elements to a journey of growth and transformation can make it be a rite of passage. Chapter XI holds more information about classical rites of passage. I recommend reading this chapter before you walk if you are considering making your Camino be such a rite.

After you have walked, you may wish to do further study. The classic texts on rites of passage by Joseph Campbell, Mircea Eliade, Arnold van Gennep, Victor Turner and Alexander John Shaia, are listed in Resources at the back of this book. These works may serve to help you understand what you have experienced.

Now—Only Now

The Camino invites you to examine the West's unhealthy relationship with time. Western culture emphasizes efficiency and production. Westerners want to know when something (whatever that something is) will be ready and the sooner the better! On the other hand, Spain and the Camino move to a far different rhythm. Relationships and a sense of timelessness are paramount. Relax. Breathe. No worry. No pressure.

Even before you leave, begin practicing how to live in the now. Regardless of where you are in your life, the practice of living in the "now" matures with dedication, repetition and resilience in the face of lapses. Commit to slow down, take deep breaths, see what is around you and feel all of your feelings.

On the Camino and beyond, use a mantra such as: "I am here." Repeat each word slowly and with intent. *I . . . AM . . . HERE.*

To read more about mindfulness and walking meditation, see Thich Nhat Hanh's exquisitely simple books listed in *Resources.*

Visualize Arriving Home

As with every suggestion in this book, use them (or not) to serve you and your Camino. With this visualization, some will wish to imagine the moment of arriving home in great detail. Others might want to use this visualization to get a general impression.

In whatever way you do this, please spend at least a bit of time thinking about your arrival home. Doing this before leaving is counter-intuitive, but you are very likely to appreciate its value when you do return home.

> *Take a few quiet moments to see yourself returning home. Visualize the mode of transportation*

that will bring you back (plane, train, bus, car or walking). See yourself rising from your seat and walking into the terminal. Who do you want to be there to greet you, if anyone?

Visualize yourself arriving at your home or apartment. Who is there? Anyone? What is the atmosphere like? Are you wanting to be met with a boisterous festive gathering or a quiet time with a few selected relatives or close friends? If you would like a gathering, do you see yourself at your home, the house of a relative or close friend, at a café, or in nature? If in nature, are you desiring the solace of mountains, forest, beach, or desert? Do you imagine an extended time there before re-entering day-to-day life?

Who, if anyone, do you see sharing this space with you? Do you see yourself alone or in conversation with a companion?

And what type of activities appeal to you: writing in your journal, reading previous entries or others' Camino stories, idly sitting, hiking, swimming, sorting through photographs, or perhaps making simple pieces of art, like a collage?

This initial visualization is simply a first look at what you may wish upon returning home. While it is important to consider and even do some minimal preparation for your homecoming before you depart, the Camino may well change your needs and initial thoughts. Hold lightly what you see in this visualization.

Discuss with whoever is likely to meet you on your return what type of return you think you may want (quiet, boisterous, many friends, few, one, none). Especially let them know what type of return you probably do not want. Ask them to respect your wishes. Emphasize that you will communicate with them in more detail late in your walk as your own needs/wishes become clear.

If you are married, in a committed relationship, a parent, or part of a covenanted community, mutual negotiation will be necessary. Discuss and agree how much time you will need for your initial adjustment to being home again.

After a lengthy Camino, I need a *minimum* of 72 hours. The amount of time you need, or can realistically take, will depend on many variables. However, please consider that you are not fully home when you walk back in the door.

Late in your walk, you will have a much clearer sense of the type of homecoming you personally need. This will be the time to communicate with those planning to meet you. No matter how well family and friends think they know you, they cannot know what your needs will be on homecoming.

If the Camino has been a true rite of passage, you will return in a different state than you left, and no one, including you, knows exactly what state that will be. Being forced to accept someone else's idea of what you need or want upon your return can be painful, and can even hurt your relationship with a spouse, a friend or a relative.

View the film Cast Away (2000) with Tom Hanks. The story conveys the four parts of every deep journey. Pay particular attention to the main character's unease and bewilderment at a party given to celebrate his return.

How does this scene strike you as you prepare to depart for the Camino? Does it seem accurate? Overly dramatic? Confusing? For many (though not all) returning pilgrims, this scene holds a powerful, and often unrecognized emotional truth.

A Message for Family and Friends

Share the following message with close friends, family and whoever might meet you on your return. Feel free to place these thoughts in your own words if you prefer, but regardless of how you share it, it is critically important that those whom you hold close are made aware of these needs.

The Camino is neither a holiday nor a vacation. Though enjoyable, it is arduous work, and

15

potentially a rite of passage that will change a pilgrim in significant ways. Especially if a pilgrim is intending the walk as a rite of passage, she or he cannot know beforehand what the experience will be, what will be the impact, or how it might change him or her. No matter how well you think you know your soon-to-be-pilgrim, you cannot know how she or he will change, nor can you know their needs upon their return.

Further, a pilgrim upon homecoming will most likely experience a fair amount of bewilderment. They will need time back in their ordinary life before they are able to make sense of the Camino, its impact and meaning. To the pilgrim, the effects and changes are usually subtle. New thoughts and attitudes only become clear once a pilgrim is back in familiar surroundings and realize they are experiencing usual events quite differently.

Some returning pilgrims need a great deal of space, patience and time to explore who they are now. Others have an even higher need to talk as they verbally process the experience. Either response can bring up various feelings (anger, impatience, frustration, envy) in those closest to a pilgrim because of her or his need for distance or increased closeness while processing their experience.

Try to view the returning pilgrim's bewilderment and questioning as an invitation for your own reflection. What areas in your own life do you wish to change? Even though you were not engaged directly in the walking, know that through the returning pilgrim the Camino invites your growth as well. Be open to change— change in your relationship with the returning pilgrim, and your own growth.

After sharing this message, consider inviting close friends and family to watch and discuss together a film or films about the Camino. The next section holds two film suggestions.

Watch Films with Family and Friends

Watching documentary films on the Camino can be a significant help to family and friends as they begin to appreciate the impact of your experience. If family and friends agree, perhaps watch the film/s together and discuss.

There are many movies and documentaries on the Camino. I highly recommend beginning with these two: *Walking the Camino: Six Ways to Santiago* and *The Way by Mark Shea*. Both are listed in *Resources* at the back of this book.

I have not mentioned Martin Sheen's movie, *The Way*. This is an entertaining fictionalized account. Enjoy it. Yet for family and friends, documentary film is a better support for them to understand what you may truly experience.

Alternately, some family and friends may prefer to watch films while you are walking, and then to re-watch with you after you have returned. Regardless when films may be watched, your providing a specific list of Camino films is an important support.

Depending on time and resources, consider purchasing copies and gifting them to family and friends to be watched at their leisure.

Remembered in Thought

Every pilgrim can benefit from having someone who holds you daily in good thought and/or prayer while you walk.

Who might be your person? Think of someone who perhaps has a daily meditation or prayer practice. In asking this person to hold you in daily thought, it is important that you *know* they take your request seriously and will not forget.

Trusted Companion / Mentor

One of your most important steps is the choice of a trusted companion or mentor with whom to share your Camino story in-depth upon your return. This person could be the same or someone different from the one who is holding you in daily thought. If you are walking as a rite of passage, having this companion or mentor in place is an essential element.

In choosing your companion/mentor, ask someone with whom you are at ease, and can trust to not judge you if you share things that are personally embarrassing or intimate in nature.

It is imperative that you have full confidence in this individual's ability to maintain confidentiality, and their ability to hear of your painful experiences without trying to fix you or resolve your pain.

This person needs to be both able and willing to repeatedly listen to your stories for weeks, months and possibly even years. Telling the stories is a way *to remember to remember.*

Repeated telling helps deepen your awareness of the lessons you are learning, marking subtle yet significant shifts in your understanding. Recounting your Camino in the presence of your companion/mentor is one of the most important, if not the most important, work of the return. Storytelling in the presence of trust, respect and love grounds and integrates the Camino's lessons into your everyday life.

If no one comes to mind as a good choice before you walk, don't worry and *please do not select someone you think might be a good choice.* You must know from your core that an individual is the right choice.

If you do not find that person before you leave, trust that you will meet her or him at the right moment. It may be someone you cross paths with on the Camino, or even discover after you arrive back home. Trust and wait.

Face-to-face sharing with your companion/ mentor is best. But, if you are not able to meet in person (perhaps they live some distance from you), consider a video calling service (Skype, Zoom, FaceTime etc.)

Seeing each other's face, even by video, is often the type of connection needed for deeper sharing to unfold.

Record A Significant Dream

Once you have made the commitment to walk the Camino, and/or shortly before you leave for the Camino, you may have a nightly dream that grabs your attention. If this happens, capture as much detail about the dream as you can remember.

It is important to write—or voice record—the dream in the present tense rather than a report about something that happened in the past, even if just minutes ago.

Record the details, especially any feelings you experience as if the dream is happening right now. Do not be concerned about interpreting the dream. It is entirely possible and quite likely that many and various meanings will come to you over time, and especially as you walk.

For more on working with dreams, see Robert Bosnak's book, *A Little Course in Dreams* listed in *Resources*. The book is an easy, non-technical read with many practical suggestions.

Letter to Yourself "Before You Walk"

When it is almost time to depart for the Camino, write a letter to yourself, seal it and leave it behind. (Alternatively, make a voice recording.) Put the letter or recording in a secure place that will be accessible to you within a few days of returning home. If you choose, you might also leave it with your companion/mentor.

In this letter or recording, recount your thoughts and feelings.

- How did the idea of walking the Camino come to you?

- How did you make the decision to walk?
- What has your preparation (or lack of it) been like?
- With departure soon, what are your thoughts, feelings, concerns, hopes, and dreams for this Camino?
- What do you want to remember after you return home about the person you are right now before you begin walking?

Use of Smartphone or Tablet

Whether to walk with a mobile, smartphone or tablet is a personal choice and will have a significant impact on your experience.

On the one hand, these devices offer ease and convenience as well as saving on weight and space. They have many uses: a built-in camera, music, GPS, torch/flashlight, weather report, medic alert, meditation timer, alarm clock, voice recorder, and eBooks/audiobooks.

On the other hand, these devices bring the world to you at every moment—world news, weather and sports, texts, ads, voice messages and calls from friends and family. How much contact with the *outer* world is beneficial to the experience that you want?

Walking with one of these devices switched on definitely hinders your experience of *now*. With a device simply turned on, your nervous system is primed and ready. A ring or a ding, even unanswered, and you are pulled elsewhere. The luxurious sense of *now* slips away.

If you are walking as a rite of passage, maintaining liminal space or little contact with the outside world is important. My first recommendation is to not carry a device at all. Simply having it with you, you are tethered to the outside world. Not having one is a significant help to your experience of living outside of time.

I understand there are many good reasons to walk with a device, including safety and emergency help if you are walking alone. My second recommendation is to carry a device, but limit where and how much you use it. As you walk, keep it switched off or switch it to airplane mode, which does not allow for calling, texting, emailing or internet use, but continues to give you access to the torch, voice recorder, music, etc.

As a general rule, keep the device in the off position or airplane mode, switching it on only to accomplish a time limited task. Perhaps, set an alarm for 15 minutes before checking texts, email or Facebook etc. each evening or every few days.

Prepare family and friends for how and when they may reach you, if at all. Tell them whether you welcome receiving chatty messages or prefer they only contact you with a pressing need.

Let them know the time of day in Spain when you are likely to check for messages. As there is little time in the mornings before you need to depart an albergue (if this is where you are staying), late afternoon through the evening is usually when pilgrims check and respond to messages.

On the YouTube film, The Smart Camino: Pilgrimage in the Internet Age (https://youtu.be/difuizJGPcQ), Nancy Frey, PhD discusses the impact of social media, mobiles etc. on the Camino. Her 1993 doctoral dissertation on the Camino is listed in Resources at the back of this book.

Send-Off

Shortly before you depart, gather with your companion or mentor, and perhaps share the letter you wrote to yourself with this person (and probably this is the *only* person to share it with).

If you already have your shell and/or pilgrim credencial, consider asking this person to take them in their hands, hold them for a moment, bless them silently or aloud with words, and to speak a good wish or prayer for your journey.

Another person to see before leaving is the one who will be holding you in special daily remembrance and prayer as you walk.

You may also wish to gather with your closest friends/family, especially those you would expect to greet you immediately upon homecoming.

Share with them your thoughts and feelings as you are about to leave. Ask for their good wishes and prayers, and their daily remembrance (thoughts and prayers) of you as you walk.

Key Actions as You Prepare to Leave

- Consider your return before you leave. Doing this will give you added benefit upon your homecoming.
- On the Camino, as with the many suggestions in this book, remember to pass by what you do not love.
- You cannot know what awaits you nor how the Camino will change you.
- The question, "Why am I walking?" has many answers. The best ones may not arrive until sometime *after* your return home.
- A friend holding you daily in good thought and prayer as you walk is pure gold.
- If you wish your Camino to be a rite of passage, having a companion or mentor who awaits your return is an important element.

*Now, quiet your mind
and go have an incredible Camino!*

III

AS YOU WALK

The first thing to do is to lift your foot.
Breathe in.
Put your foot down in front of you,
first your heel and then your toes.
Breathe out.

Feel your feet solid on the Earth.
You have already arrived.

Thich Nhat Hanh
How to Walk

Each Day, with Each Step...

As you walk, perhaps especially each morning as you
put on your "boots," take a few intentional breaths and
remind yourself of the freedom and the honor to join
with pilgrims of all ages, from across the globe, taking time away from day to day life, to walk, reflect and
perhaps pray. What a joy, a privilege it is to breathe, to
be alive, to be here, and to walk.

Give gratitude for all the pilgrims who have walked
before, for your personal ancestors, for your teachers,
family, friends and co-workers. Say a prayer—or send
a good wish—to all pilgrims who are on the road with

you today, and all who will come after you tomorrow and the many tomorrows after that.

Lastly as you take your first step each morning, remind yourself of the pilgrim motto: My job today is to walk and be grateful.

Many have a mistaken notion of pilgrim gratitude. It is not a practice of reflecting on the day, recounting all the pleasant things that have happened. Pilgrim gratitude is receiving whatever happens with a sense of gratitude regardless of circumstance.

How may I receive untoward events with gratitude? Vaclev Havel, author and former Czech president, said: "Hope is not the conviction that something will turn out well, but the certainty that something makes sense, regardless of how it turns out."

Attempt to hold untoward experiences as meaningful and have gratitude for the answers that will eventually arrive.

Anonymity

As an author and speaker, when I walked my first Camino, I wanted to step outside these roles and the expectations placed on them by the public. I did not want to talk about my books or speaking or professional life. I told no one who I was or what I did for a living until near the end of my walk.

—

Also, I chose a different name for myself. My pilgrim name had a personal meaning for me at that point in my life but was not associated with me in any other way.

Walking the Camino affords you a rare opportunity to step out of your history, story, and even name. Perhaps you are in a profession with great public expectations, and you would like to simply be a person, a pilgrim. Or maybe you are feeling trapped in a role and want to break free.

You can choose to tell any story about your life and yourself that you may wish. I am not suggesting telling falsehoods. The Camino is an opportunity to explore parts of yourself that perhaps have remained more hidden, maybe even hidden from yourself. Is there an alternate story of you that is waiting to be explored?

Often on the Camino, pilgrims choose a "Camino name" for themselves, or are given a humorous one by other pilgrims. These names usually come from a quality or quirk that you have, or a story that happens to you as you walk.

Pilgrims have been known to prefer giving themselves a name rather than wait for it to be given by others! Is there a name—humorous or meaningful—that you wish to take for yourself as you walk? Listen inside.

In a rite of passage, initiates often receive a new name that in some way signifies one's growth, change or transformation. As you walk, does a new name come to you? If yes, consider a re-naming ritual at an appropriate place and time, i.e. a forest, stream, mountain, beach, Santiago, your turn-around place, or back home.

Questions to Ask Yourself

I would like to beg you ... as well as I can, to have patience with everything unresolved in your heart and to try to love the questions themselves as if they were locked rooms or books written in a very foreign language. Don't search for the answers, which could not be given to you now, because you would not be able to live them.

And the point is to live everything. Live the questions now. Perhaps then, someday far in the future, you will gradually, without even noticing it, live your way into the answer.

Rainer Maria Rilke
Letters to a Young Poet

Undoubtedly the question, "Why are you walking?" is the most asked on the Camino. And within that question lies another: What do you hope to get out of this walk? Or, what does the Camino mean to you?

Before you answer this or any question asked of you on the Camino, realize that you have the power of choice. You may choose to answer or not answer any question about your life asked of you by another.

Moment by moment choose the level of socializing that is right for you at *this* moment, *this* day, etc.

Bring any search for the right answer to a full stop. Like water in one's palm, let your thoughts gently pass through. Be playful with your thinking and avoid getting too serious or staid.

Don't fall into the trap of believing that there is just one right answer. Ask yourself daily, "Why am I walking?" And, as a Buddhist might advise: "Let the answers come. Let the answers go." Don't grasp or judge them. Notice how your response/s shift depending on who asks, the time of day or night, your location and your energy level.

Practice being in the moment. This will save you time, alleviate an enormous amount of frustration, and increase your ability to experience joy. Trying to figure out the why and what of your Camino as you walk is futile.

In almost every instance, you will not know the why or what until near your turn around place, or even more likely not until after you return home. Clarity arrives in its own time.

Learn how to be curious about yourself and become comfortable with uncertainty. To be at ease with "not knowing" is a sign of one's growing maturity.

Attempt to relax in the midst of experiencing difficulties or swirling thoughts. Practice loving these moments. Each time your mind or body screams to know the answer, gently repeat to yourself: "There is time. There is time. There is time." Turn your walk into a type of meditation—eyes open, mind still, feet moving.

Another question to perhaps ask yourself daily is: "What is the purpose of my life—now?" Don't expect an immediate answer. Simply continue to ask yourself the question.

Ask it as you walk. Ask it as you reach your turn-around place. Ask it when you return home. Keep asking it. At some point an answer will arrive that surprises you with its energy, impact and ring of truth. When such an answer arrives, don't delay in writing it down or speaking into a voice recorder.

Another aid in remembering it is to immediately free associate the answer with an image, picture or symbol. Such a deep answer usually carries a great deal of energy, and you can easily delude yourself into believing you will never forget this. Yet if the answer is not quickly recorded in some way, you *will* forget and perhaps as quickly as within an hour or two.

If such an answer comes while walking, don't even wait until the next village. Pause, and capture it in the moment.

—

The Camino as Meditation and Prayer

When walking, I begin each day with a few minutes of quiet dedication using one of these prayers or poems. Each evening, I take a moment to review my day through the prism of that morning's prayer/poem.

I ask that I may be given
the appropriate difficulties and sufferings on this
journey
so that my heart may be awakened,
and my practice of compassion and liberation
for all beings may be fulfilled.

Buddhist intention before meditation

All shall be well,
and all manner of thing shall be well.

Juliana of Norwich / *Showings*

In beauty I walk
With beauty before me I walk
With beauty behind me I walk
With beauty above me I walk
With beauty around me I walk
It has become beauty—again
Today I will walk out
Today everything negative will leave me
I will be as I was before
I will have a cool breeze over my body
I will have a light body,

Alexander John Shaia

I will be happy forever, nothing will hinder me
I walk with beauty before me
I walk with beauty behind me
I walk with beauty below me
I walk with beauty above me
I walk with beauty around me
My words will be beautiful

In beauty all day long may I walk
Through the returning seasons, may I walk
On the trail marked with pollen may I walk
With dew about my feet, may I walk
With beauty before me, may I walk
With beauty behind me, may I walk
With beauty below me, may I walk
With beauty above me, may I walk
With beauty all around me, may I walk
In old age wandering on a trail of beauty,
lively may I walk
In old age wandering on a trail of beauty,
living again, may I walk
My words will be beautiful.

Navajo Chant, "Walking in Beauty"
—*Blessing Way Ceremony*

I said to my soul, be still
and wait without hope,
for hope would be hope for the wrong thing:
wait without love,
for love would be love of the wrong thing;
there is yet faith,

but the faith and the love are all in the waiting.
Wait without thought,
for you are not ready for thought:
So the darkness shall be the light,
and the stillness the dancing.

T.S. Eliot
East Coker, Four Quartets

Dear God, (Spirit, Christ, Higher Power...)

I have no idea where I am going. I do not see the road
ahead of me. I cannot know for certain where it will
end. Nor do I really know myself, and the fact that I
think I am following your Will does not mean that I
am actually doing so.

But I believe my desire to please you does in fact please
you. And I hope that I have that desire in all that I am
doing. I hope that I will never do anything apart from
that desire. And I know that if I do this You will lead me
by the right road though I may know nothing about it.

Therefore, I will trust You always though I may seem
to be lost and in the shadow of death. I will not fear,
for You are ever with me and You will never leave me
to face my perils alone.

Prayer of Thomas Merton

O what a miracle to be awake
inside [my] breathing.

Hildegard of Bingen

This being human is a guest house
Every morning a new arrival.
A joy, a depression, a meanness,
some momentary awareness comes
as an unexpected visitor.
Welcome and entertain them all!
Even if they are a crowd of sorrows,
who violently sweep your house
empty of its furniture,
still, treat each guest honorably.
He may be clearing you out
for some new delight.
The dark thought, the shame, the malice.
meet them at the door laughing
and invite them in.
Be grateful for whatever comes.
because each has been sent
as a guide from beyond.

Rumi
The Guest House

Difficulties and obstacles on the Camino wear many guises. Pilgrims are all too familiar with the pain of blisters, body aches or that person (another pilgrim, bar owner, hospitalero, etc.) who gets under the skin. However, the practice of keeping the mind quiet, in the midst of unwanted visitors, can be equally vexing.

The Guest House, by the 13th century poet, philosopher Rumi, eloquently speaks to this practice of welcoming each visitor.

As you begin walking each day, ask yourself:

"What has arrived this morning?"

Follow this, by expressing your welcome.

In the evening, review the day and ask yourself:

"What happened today with what arrived this morning?"

Surprised by Emotion

Your experiences on the Camino are greatly influenced by your personality. Do you tend to be emotional? Feeling type? Critical thinker? Stoic?

Regardless, you may find yourself caught unaware by surging emotion.

Like the Rumi poem, something arrives in a flash. Suddenly, caught by beauty, tears stream. Suddenly, caught by grief, tears stream. Suddenly, hilarious laughter. Suddenly, boiling anger. Suddenly, bliss. Suddenly, a calm. Allow each emotion to come. Know also that in time, each will pass.

Everything Belongs

Dark Madonna, San Martin de Tours de Fromista Fromista, Palencia, Spain

Black Madonna of Montserrat reproduction in side chapel, Santiago de Compostela Cathedral, Galicia, Spain

Along the Camino Frances, there are churches where you may visit images of a Dark or Black Madonna (including Pamplona, Logrono, Fromista, Villavante, Astorga, Ponferrada, and Santiago). Sadly, many dark Madonnas in Spain were painted over and made light-skinned in the centuries since the Enlightenment.

The significance of the dark holy earthy feminine is deep and myriad. One aspect of particular importance is that she is the needed counterbalance to the one-sided belief that an authentic life (psychologically or spiritually) is found in seeking ever more light.

Nothing could be more limiting or hurtful to us. Everything belongs! We need dark and light. Both elements are good and critically necessary for our growth. The need is for both to be in right relationship or proportion to each other.

Wendell Berry, poet and farmer, writes:

To go in the dark with a light
is to know the light.
To know the dark, go dark.
Go without sight,
and find that the dark, too, blooms and sings,
and is traveled by dark feet and dark wings.

poem, *To Know the Dark*
from *The Selected Poems of Wendell Berry*, 1999

David Whyte echoes a similar sentiment in his poem, *Sweet Darkness*:

Sometimes it takes darkness and the sweet
Confinement of your aloneness
to learn
anything or anyone
that does not bring you alive
is too small for you.

David Whyte
from *River Flow*

For me, Spain's dark Madonnas are a tangible reminder that all of life is sacred, and that our best efforts will

be in our attempts to love what is, especially when—
what is—is a "dark" emotion, thought, or moment.

Language Shapes Experience

Language largely shapes our experience and expectations. A significant benefit to your entire Camino will
be "writing" the following on your mind and heart:

*Where I stop walking is not my destination. My desti-
nation is "here," "home," and a life renewed.*

*My turn-around place is where the second half of the
Camino begins.*

Use language in a way that reminds you no city or location on a map is your destination, not Santiago, Fisterra
or Muxia. And the place where you stop walking is not
the end but only where you *turn around*, and begin the
Camino's second half, the journey home.

There is a small but increasing number of pilgrims who
having reached Santiago or the Sea, walk back to where
they started, or even to their own homes. Of course, this
was the experience of most pilgrims before the modern
age.

Today, pilgrims largely return by planes, trains and
buses. These luxuries should not keep you from the
awareness that the Camino is *from* home *back to* home.

—

In terms of a rite of passage, the return home is the longest and most emotionally arduous of the entire journey and lasts far longer than the time it takes to physically travel back to your home.

Singing-Chanting

As an aid to staying in the *now*, diminishing thesense of any destination, you might use a Plum Village chant as you walk. See YouTube: *Plum Village Songs All Together.*

The songs are inspired by Thich Nhat Hanh, a Buddhist monk and founder of Plum Village in France. Here are the lyrics of three chants especially suited to the time of walking:

I Have Arrived

I have arrived, I am home.
In the here and in the now.
I am solid. I am free.
In the ultimate I dwell.

Happiness is Here and Now

Happiness is here and now
I have dropped my worries
Nowhere to go
Nothing to do
No longer in a hurry.
Happiness is here and now

I have dropped my worries
Somewhere to go
Something to do
But not in a hurry.

Been Traveling a Day

Been traveling a day,
Been traveling a year
Been traveling a lifetime
To find my way home
Home is where the heart is,
Home is where the heart is
Home is where the heart is
My heart is with you

Thich Nhat Hanh's book, *How to Walk*, is a short, simple read. See *Resources* at the back of this book.

IV

ARRIVING AT THE CATHEDRAL
(The Shrine)

... as if, all along, you had thought the end point might be a city with golden towers, and cheering crowds, and turning the corner at what you thought was the end of the road, you found just a simple reflection, and a clear revelation, and beneath it another invitation... and the road still stretching on.

David Whyte
from the poem, *Santiago*

Refrain from Expectation

Along with the sweat and grind of daily walks, undoubtedly there will be moments of joy (perhaps even bliss), of connection, friendship and even a growing sense of life purpose as you journey along the Camino. However, refrain from any expectation of what you may feel upon arriving at the Cathedral in Santiago.

This may be the place where it all comes together, you feel fulfilled, and your journey makes sense. However, it could just as well be the place where it all falls apart and you realize that you are seeking something other than what the Cathedral or Santiago offers you.

Have no expectation, but rather simply make note of your feelings and reactions while you are there. You may find yourself elated, relieved, proud, tearful or blissed in the presence of dear friends.

On the other hand, you may be depressed, disillusio-ned, stoic, angry, sad, or feeling very alone. Moreover, you are likely to have some combination of these fee-lings, or you may even experience all of them at once.

I have stood in the Cathedral many times and observed every one of these responses. Some pilgrims look abso-lutely beatific—as if suddenly overtaken by the presen-ce of the Holy. But, too often, I have seen looks of see-ming emptiness and bewilderment on pilgrim faces. I have even seen what I would describe as seething anger.

Whatever feelings arise for you upon arrival, simply note them and come back to the place of refraining from expectation.

If you are experiencing joy or even bliss at being in the Cathedral, please be mindful that this may not be true for the person next to you. And if you are experien-cing difficult or troubling emotions, especially in the Cathedral, being around others who appear to be ha-ppy or in a state of bliss could exacerbate your sense of unease, disappointment and isolation.

I have often heard pilgrims at the Cathedral say with dripping sarcasm, "I walked all this way for *this*?" If

—

any of this proves true for you, then visiting the Saint's tomb, hugging his statue, or attending the Pilgrims' Mass may be empty rituals that strike deep chords of bitterness and cynicism.

Be mindful of two things. Pass by what you do not love. And a pilgrim's work is to be respectful of self and others. Allow each the space to experience her or his own truth.

Each of us is unique; so, too will be your personal reaction to various places and types of experiences on the Camino. Like the gentle striking of a bell, the repeated counsel throughout this book is to hold your thoughts and feelings lightly, playfully and without judgment. They are *your* truth, and yours alone.

And remember the destination is not Cathedral Square, Fisterra or Muxia. Wherever you stop walking is merely your turn-around place. Your journey continues and the road stretches before you. Pick up your pack and continue to walk *your* Camino.

Santiago, Santiago, Santiago

The city is a complex experience. After days, weeks, months in smaller towns, in the quiet of nature and surrounded by fellow pilgrims, Santiago's bustling largess can be overwhelming.

Cathedral square, souvenir shops and cafes can appear as a crowded bazaar. Merchants hawking their wares and countless tourists taking pictures of pilgrims might lift your spirit or be a trial to your hard won serenity.

While walking across long stretches of the Camino, stopping in smaller villages and perhaps finding a band of fellow pilgrims who look out for each other, a lovely sense of trust and safety arises.

However, entering Santiago's Cathedral Square, you need to be aware that not everyone you encounter will be trustworthy. Pickpockets are a bit more prevalent here and even inside the Cathedral.

You may find your senses overwhelmed by the festive gathering of pilgrims, including ones that you thought you might never see again. However, be vigilant. Guard yourself against being a victim of those who don't have your best interest in mind.

Embrace Cathedral Square and the city for what they are. Do not attempt to remake them. If you find yourself buoyed and enjoying the bustle and sweet company of fellow pilgrims, stay awhile. But, if you become weary or cynical at seeing what seems the crass business of pilgrimage, move on to the Sea or an earlier place on the Camino that nurtured and energized you.

—

Santiago may be a highlight of your Camino, your worst nightmare or something in between.

Whatever your reaction to Santiago and The Cathedral, know you are not alone. Whatever your feelings and reactions, they are valid, and have been experienced by countless pilgrims before you.

V

ONCE WALKING HAS ENDED

The Way has no end. But our steps, yes.

Anonymous
Sign on the Camino

*How will you remember to remember
when you return home?*

Phil Cousineau
The Art of Pilgrimage

Turn-Around Place

Wherever it is that you end your walk westward—
Santiago, Fisterra, Muxia or another place—this location is your turn-around place.

This place is both an ending and a beginning. It com-
pletes the westward journey and is also the start of the
Camino's second half, the journey home. It is therefore
a place for reflection, rest, and celebration on all that
the Camino has been to date, a place for anticipation
of what is to come as you return home, and a place
of some bewilderment as you say goodbye to the ever
present yellow arrows pointing westward, and perhaps
begin to wonder, "What is my direction now?"

Alexander John Shaia

My assumption is that most of you are not walking back home. Before the invention of the train, pilgrims returned home either on foot or horseback. The second half of their Camino was just as arduous (if not more so) than the first half.

Yet the weeks to months of walking back home held a gift that is missing for the contemporary pilgrim. The lengthy time and physical exertion allowed for a deepening reflection on what had happened and continued to happen as they walked toward home. Equally, the pilgrim would have the time to look ahead, anticipate homecoming and prepare themselves to see family and friends again.

Stay at your turn-around-place anywhere from a few days to a week or longer. Do *not* rush straight to the airport/train station without the opportunity to remember, record, and begin to digest all that has happened as you walked, as well as to consider your return and homecoming.

Wherever you are, linger awhile. Enjoy the convivial atmosphere of pilgrims in Santiago, the serene sunsets of Fisterra or the ancient field of rock in Muxia. However, resist any gesture or ritual that says the journey is complete.

Of late, pilgrims have begun to burn their clothes below the lighthouse at Fisterra as the sun sets over the ocean. I am not a fan of this gesture for it tends to say the Camino is over. The reality is that you are not at the end of the Camino, only the end of the first half.

Again, I have heard from too many pilgrims who burned their clothes here to celebrate their accomplished ending, and then returned home only to be shocked by their depression and unease. Something deep in us knows that this is a turn-around place, half a Camino, not an end.

It's true that many Medieval pilgrims burned their clothes at a designated place near the Cathedral. At first the fires were set outside the North Entrance. Once a fountain was built there, the roof became the designated place. Were pilgrims burning their clothes to signify the end of their Camino? Hardly. They had an entire return journey ahead. For them, the burning was to prevent the spreading of lice.

To participate in a ritual that says to yourself and others that your Camino has come to an end is to participate in a falsehood. It is not an emotional help to the arduous journey ahead as you return home. You may need those clothes metaphorically, if not literally, as a reminder of the Camino's first half, and the commitment required to truly effect change once back at home.

The ritual of burning clothes at the right moment carries great truth and power. One effective moment would be to have a fire near the time of your Gathering, months after returning home. See *Chapter X, Closure: Fire— Gathering—Service* for more details.

However, there may be something that you wish to let go of, or leave behind here, or even burn. Are there one or two small items that signify a part of you that has begun to die or change as you walked? Whatever that *death* may be, its true passing will only be evident by the choices you make once you are back home. Here at the turn-around place, make a gesture that states your commitment to live differently.

Physical Cool Down

For today's pilgrim it is vitally important to create a cool down time of rest and reflection before home-coming. Just as an athlete requires a period of cooling down immediately following intense exertion, the Camino pilgrim does as well. At the turn-around-place, your body is primed for walking long distances and for a higher caloric intake needed to sustain lengthy exercise.

During this time in-between the end of lengthy walking and your return home, facilitate a physical cool down. Rather than just stopping lengthy daily walks, continue walking each day for an hour or two, along with an intentional decrease in calories. If you are so inclined and if medically appropriate for you, consider a one or two day fast from solid foods, consuming only liquids and juices. If you are accustomed to a more intense food cleanse, consider beginning it now, at your turn-around place.

In whatever way, from exercise to food intake to rest, allow your body to gradually adjust to the change in your daily routine.

Questions Rush In

As you pause and rest, the turn-around place is often where you will become aware of a host of feelings ranging from contentment, joy, pride and relief, to sadness, numbness and defeat. This is also the place where the feelings of uncertainty and isolation can overwhelm you. At this pivotal moment between the first and second halves of the Camino, it is not uncommon to fear the loss of everything you gained on the Camino when you return home.

You may be concerned that family and friends won't understand your experience, that you won't be able to feel the type of presence, aliveness and authenticity you experienced while walking, or that life back home will seem shallow by comparison. It is also perfectly normal at this point on your journey to find yourself asking questions such as:

- What are the gifts I received as I walked? New attitudes? Life lessons? Friendships?
- In returning home, will I leave behind my discoveries and learnings?
- What will life back home be like? Will it feel dull and mundane? Can I face it? Or will it feel renewed, more vital?

- Where is the "something" more?
- I spent all of that time, effort and money for *this*?
- Is there a new life plan? Did I miss it?

Having many questions, even conflicting questions, at this point is usual and to be expected. As you end long hours of walking and begin to physically slow, the mind usually roars back, perhaps even in overdrive.

Noticing your many questions, does not mean you need to have answers. Allow yourself to celebrate, rest, remember, and record. Answers will come in due time, but usually not until you have been back home awhile.

A Dream

As you near your turn-around place, have you experienced an impactful nightly dream that was inspiring, disturbing, or mysterious?

Recall the dream with as much detail as you are able, especially feelings you remember having, and images you remember seeing in the dream. Again, record the dream, in writing or by voice recorder, using present tense. Every aspect of a dream has meaning; however, for right now simply journal what you remember.

Don't be concerned about interpreting the dream's meaning—allow the pulsing energy of the dream to move you. Notice where or what the dream's energy touches inside you. Where do you feel it in your body?

What moment/place on your Camino holds energy that is similar to the energy in your dream? Give your dream a title. Play with the words and images. Dreams are full of puns, look for them.

For more on dream work, see the book, *A Little Course in Dreams*, by Robert Bosnak listed in *Resources*. His writing is non-technical, easily accessible with many practical suggestions.

Your Journal

The emotion of reaching Santiago, the Cathedral or your turn-around place often crowds out self-reflection and time spent with your journal, either written or spoken.

As you rest, make those entries that have been waiting a while. This is also an appropriate time to look back over your journal, re-read certain passages or perhaps even read your journal in its entirety.

Sharing with Other Pilgrims

As you rest, record and begin to digest your experiences, you naturally may want to share your thoughts with other pilgrims. Sharing can be mutually beneficial, sparking your own memory of forgotten experiences, even significant experiences, reinforcing lessons learned, etc.

However, some types of sharing can be detrimental to your journey. Determine your own level of comfort. How much privacy do you need? Which stories or lessons are appropriate for you to share? Which stories reveal too much for you to be at ease sharing with a fellow pilgrim?

Additionally, be cautious of sharing vulnerable growing edges with another if you are not confident of their having a non-judgmental attitude. If another pilgrim were to criticize you or make a harsh judgment, it could potentially deter you from continued personal growth.

Write Yourself a Second Letter

After you have rested and feel a bit more caught up, begin to write yourself a second letter. (Were you able to write yourself one before leaving?)

In this letter, share the many gifts, essential truths, significant moments, lessons and people from this Camino that have touched you, inspired you, awakened joy, repulsed you and/or brought you to your knees.

Take as much time as you need to write your thoughts, but it is important that you finish it before leaving for home. When you feel the letter is complete, seal it and put it somewhere protected from weather. Then mark a date in your diary/calendar about 40–60 days after you return home.

If you are the type of person who doesn't refer to a calendar often, then once home, give the letter to your companion/mentor, asking them to return the letter to you on or shortly before the date you have chosen to read it. Set aside a quiet time for yourself on that date to read your letter.

Consider reading it the first time in the presence of your companion/mentor. Your writing should only be shared with someone in whom you have the utmost confidence they can hear your letter without judgment or criticism. This may or may not be a spouse, close friend or family member.

Re-Naming

In a classic rite of passage, an initiate is often given a new name that in someway signifies one's growth, change or transformation.

As you walked, arrived in Santiago, or at your turn-around place, has a new name for yourself come to you?

If yes, consider the place and time for a re-naming ritual. Here in Spain? Once back home? What type of place—forest, stream, mountain, beach, a garden, home, labyrinth or personally significant chapel?

Communicate with Those at Home

Having written the second letter, now its time to seriously ponder your homecoming. Take a few quiet moments to see yourself returning home. Visualize the mode of transportation that will bring you back (plane, train, bus, car, bicycle, horse, or walking). If your mode of transportation is other than on foot, see yourself rising from your seat, and walking into the terminal. Who do you want to be there to greet you, if anyone?

See yourself arriving at your dwelling. Who is there? Anyone? What is the atmosphere like? Are you wanting to be met with a boisterous festive gathering, a quiet time with a few selected relatives/close friends, or no one? If you would like a gathering, do you see yourself at your home, the house of a relative or close friend, at a café, a park or in a more removed nature setting?

If nature, are you desiring the solace of mountains, forest, running or still water, beach or desert? If so, imagine an extended time there before re-entering day-to-day life. Who, if anyone, do you see sharing this space with you? What do you want to be doing during this time? Are you alone or in conversation with a companion?

—

What type of activities appeal to you? Writing in your journal? Reading your journal? Reading others' Camino stories? Sorting through photographs? Or, perhaps making simple pieces of art, like collage?

Compare how you saw homecoming *before* walking with how you see it now. Review the visualization about your homecoming you did before you left. The difference in your thoughts pre- and post-walk provides an early clue as to how the experience of the Camino is changing you.

Be Aware

Friends and family at home mean well. You have been gone and they most probably want to let you know how you have been missed. However, I have heard too many horror stories about a surprise party given for a returning pilgrim.

For many (not all) who are returning home from a rite of passage, a festive party soon after homecoming is probably not helpful. This type of gathering may be jarring, even disrupting your deep experience and stress your relationship with others.

A celebratory gathering a few months later is, however, quite appropriate. See *Chapter X, Closure: Fire— Gathering—Service*. With that in mind and before leaving for home, communicate your needs with those who plan to greet you upon your arrival, as well as any who plan to visit you over your first week back home.

The Second Half Begins

The first half of your Camino—preparing to walk, walking, arriving at your turn-around place, resting and reflecting—has undoubtedly taught you something of inner contentment, a joy not dependent on outer circumstance, courage, patience and perseverance. Timely! These are exactly the qualities needed as you return home, walking the Camino's second half. Ready?

NOTE: As you read the next few chapters, find the ideas that call to you, that make sense to you, and please pass by the rest. Remember to make this book an aid to your needs, and your homecoming.

VI

TRAVELING TOWARD HOME

If the path before you is clear,
you're probably on someone else's.

Joseph Campbell
The Hero's Journey

Pilgrimage is not just about leaving ordinary life. It is
much more, a process that involves stages of moving
from ordinary space into sacred space and then back
into ordinary space, from structure to non-structure
then back to structure.

Sarah York
Pilgrim Heart

How I wish there was a magic bullet to solve the riddle of re-entry. However, traveling home asks the same level of individual work as both your preparation to walk and the walk itself. The work of the return is more internal, less visible to others and often receives far less support from those around us. And there is no Pilgrim Credencial with sellos (stamps) to be collected as you travel home.

Sustainable growth and transformation do not happen while you are walking. True change depends largely on what you do as you travel back, re-enter home and the months immediately after your arrival.

If you have had the good fortune to begin planning for your return before you left, you have a head start; however, it is never too late to begin the work of homecoming.

Keep an Attitude of Walking

Maintaining an attitude of being on the Camino as you travel back and arrive home is a significant help. As Westerners, we tend to pressure ourselves to immediately "know what it all means."

On returning home we might rush to wrap up our experience, tell a great story, hold on to the highs, distance ourselves from the painful moments and have that festive gathering with family and friends. Then we begin to pack away our photos and mementos so we can get on with our lives and plan the next experience.

I urge you *not* to do your homecoming like this! Such actions de-evolve the Camino from a potentially significant rite of passage into a moment's ecstasy, an adventure trek, or a walking holiday.

Injury

Traveling home with an injury happens all too often. For Westerners, a physical injury is usually viewed as either an accident or a mistake that could have been avoided.

Yet one of the Camino's lessons is that everything has purpose and meaning. Physical injury inevitably slows your pace. The opportunity for time to reflect can be a help, keeping the Camino alive within you for a longer period of time.

Should you find yourself physically injured, reflect on what meaning your injury holds for you. Ask yourself questions like:

- What opportunity does this injury offer me?
- How is this particular wound teaching me to move in a new way or at a different pace?
- What larger message does this injury hold for me as I seek changes in my everyday life?

I had this very experience. As I stood at the Santiago airport on my way home, I slung my backpack onto the beltway at the airline counter. This is the pack that I had carried on my back for 50 days. Just as I slung it, something in my shoulder popped. The next two months were a blur of excruciating pain and choice words, bemoaning my bad luck at the very last moment. I had walked eight weeks with only a slight leg rash and a bit of an ache in my right knee. Why did this injury have to happen just as I headed home?

After arriving back in the States and receiving effective pain medication, I began to realize how the injury and resulting ache were teaching me about the emotional weight I usually carry on my shoulders. The Camino was asking me to set those burdens down. The stabbing discomfort in my shoulder kept me aware of this important lesson over many days, nights and weeks.

During those months of recovery, I became increasingly mindful of the fact that I had gone on the Camino to re-examine the habitual way I was living my life. I wanted to make different choices. The injury itself, the resulting physical ache and the slower pace brought that lesson painfully home. Over a long period of time, they served to ensure that I would remember to make new and different choices.

Sitting at the Edge

Re-entry is almost always a physical shock, but it may also be an emotional and spiritual one as well. Modern travel (plane, train, and bus) bring us home far sooner than our bodies and psyches are prepared for. Jet-lag only compounds this challenge.

A century and a half ago, a pilgrim would have weeks to months of walking to emotionally prepare for their arrival home. In more indigenous cultures, the returning pilgrim is often required to sit outside the village for two or three days before re-entering. During this time, prayers of gratitude and request are offered, along with the burning of candles, sage or incense to remove any undesirable "spirit" that may have attached to the pilgrim during the journey.

This ritual may seem odd to us, but if you recall, when astronauts returned from the Moon they were quarantined for days to make sure microbes had not attached to them, which if introduced on the planet could wreak havoc on our eco-system.

While it may not be practical for you today to literally sit outside the city limits of your home, I do suggest taking a few days or more in a solitary setting immediately upon returning home. See *Chapter VII, Homecoming*. Allow your psyche, mind and body to gradually return to equilibrium. Jet-lag is more than simply a physical condition.

Meet at a Neutral Space

If you are returning home to a spouse, significant other or close family member, consider meeting them in a neutral space, a space other than their or your own home. Why? Walking back into a familiar and intimate space immediately places you and the other in territory that has memories and expectations from the past. This is a new moment. You are in a different space, and very likely your spouse or significant friend is as well.

If possible, meet in a spacious, neutral place without other people near. Consider a nature setting, park or botanical garden. Take a walk with each other. Begin to allow your body rhythms to mesh again. In this neutral space, you will likely be able to mutually share, listen, and hear the other more freely.

Lessen the Effects of Possible Shock

In the time immediately before and after re-entering your home, shock often leads us to feel emotionally drained, cognitively dull, a general sense of being out of balance and often asking questions like: "Where am I?" "What has happened?" "What do I really believe about my life?"

Right before and immediately after arriving home, be gentle with yourself. Give yourself time, space, sleep, healthy nutritious food and physical exercise outside in nature. To further lessen the effects of shock, you might consider nurturing yourself with massage, acupuncture, yoga, art making, poetry, meditative music, and/or soothing aromas.

Especially needed during shock and re-entry, continue the practice of living in the now while holding expectations off to the side (see *Chapter II, As You Walk*).

—

I encouraged these practices as you walked so that in part you would be prepared to use them as you return home. Repeat the phrase to yourself often: "There is time. There is time."

Note your thoughts and feelings during this time of shock. Record them in some way. Having them for later recall is another help in understanding what it is that you wish to change in your life.

VII

HOMECOMING

To return to the source,
one must travel in the opposite direction.

René Daumal
from *Mount Analogue*

The 'elsewhere' is 'here'
in the immediacy of real life.

René Daumal
from *Une experience fondamentale*

Welcome Pride—Welcome Bewilderment

Homecoming is a complex tapestry with many textures, thoughts and feelings.

There can be the joyful anticipation of being reunited with friends and family as well as the physical relief of not walking long distances every day. Additionally, there is likely to be a sense of pride and accomplishment to be shared with friends and family, a sense of "I did it!" These are the emotions you rightly expect.

However, alongside these are likely to be feelings of bewilderment, loss and an inner chaos. Despite

the joy and relief, you literally are in some manner of disorientation. How could you not be? As
you walked, life moved at four to five kilometers
(3 miles) per hour for days, weeks and even months. The
simple daily repetitive routine of walking along with
limited choices created its own form of trance. As you
walked, it was as if you were in a dream state—which
you were! Returning to your day- to-day life can easily become overwhelming, especially in the West where
the pace is often frenetic with seemingly endless tasks
and a numbing amount of choices.

Walk through this time slowly and with intent. Breathe
deeply into each moment, each emotion and each
thought. As the Rumi poem says, *Welcome and entertain them all!*

Bit of Chaos

Significant life experiences impact us with energy at
high voltage, a level that our physical, emotional and
intellectual selves are not prepared to handle. Sadly,
Western culture tempts us to revel in and indulge this
energy, thereby dissipating it, rather than harnessing it
for our growth and sustainable change.

We tend to erroneously believe that the lively scintil-
lations we are feeling herald the arrival of answers to
all our questions. In reality what has happened is that
we have tapped a fresh reservoir of energy. Neither the

experience nor the energy is the answer, nor are they yet the growth we seek. The experience is simply the energy.

Its use is as fuel to help us make the changes that the walk has awakened in us. This is the primary reason I offer so many cautions about the days immediately before and after arriving home. Too much celebration and too many visitors prompt us to begin speaking of the Camino in past tense, and ultimately packing it away.

You must harness the energy to accomplish the growth and transformation you seek. Think of the energy as sun and water in right measure for crops to grow and mature. Seeds must still be planted, crops inspected, cared for, and ultimately harvested. Sun and water do not do the work, but in right measure they enable growth until harvest time.

Be at Ease

Energy, in nature and in us, oscillates between two poles (positive and negative). Think of the connecting points on a battery. This patterned movement of energy can be imagined like a pulsing figure eight.

However, the pace of the oscillations is not even and steady but varies wildly. As humans, when this fresh energy reservoir is released within, the oscillations move with great velocity.

In yoga this release is called *kundalini* and is imaged as energy shooting up the spine, moving through the seven chakra centers in the body. Depending on many personal factors, the experience of this energy may range from euphoria to deep peace to utter depression.

Though I am speaking of the arrival of this type of fresh energy as part of the return home, be vigilant. This energy may arrive at any time—as you walk, at your turn-around place, on the return, or during the time of integration once home. Likewise, the energy may arrive before you leave to walk, or not arrive for months to years after you have returned home.

When the energy does arrive, the work is not to immediately seek balance. Rather, learn to be at ease with the peaks and valleys that you experience. Soon after the energy arrives, write down or make a voice recording that captures your thoughts and feelings. As the oscillations slow, you will have a more stable and determined core from which to consider changes and new directions.

There are many practices that help you learn how to ride the waves: meditation, centering prayer, art, yoga, Tai Chi, Qigong, time in nature, and sharing about the experience in conversation with your companion/mentor and trusted friends.

These practices teach us how to be present with energy, rather than attempting to exert control over it. These practices teach us to *trust in the process, go with the flow, and not to push the river.*

NOTE: This type of energy is far more powerful than we can imagine, and it is almost impossible for our human intellect to contain it. It is largely beyond our rational control. While it does pulse and oscillate within, the energy primarily moves us in one of two directions. For most, it brings us expansive thoughts and feelings. However, some of us can plummet into a depressed-like state, feeling a tight constriction, and almost crushing sense of unworthiness.

Regardless of which of the two experiences you have, simply be with the energy, be in frequent conversation with your companion/mentor, and resist the impulse to take any particular decisive action.

After a short period of time—anywhere from a few days to a few weeks—you will begin to experience one of life's great paradoxes: the arrival of this energy has not solved your problems, but in fact has increased the chaos and tension in your life.

In reality, the energy is actually helping you experience the intellectual and emotional chasm between the vitality in your new sense of self and the lack of energy in your "old" self. You feel a growing intense dissonance between who you have been, and who you are in the process of becoming. Into this gap, life can bring pressing dilemmas that serve as trial and error opportunities, helping you learn how to use this energy in new and different ways in the midst of your everyday life.

Returning from the walk and discovering that life back home is in some manner of inner or outer chaos, does not mean the walk was a waste of time and effort. Rather, the chaos you feel upon your return means that you are right in the midst of a time of tremendous growth and transformation. The chaos is a sign that you are beginning to integrate the Camino's lessons into your everyday life.

For more about the requisite chaos at this point in a classical rite of passage, see the books of Joseph Campbell, Mircea Eliade, Arnold van Gennep, and Victor Turner, listed in *Resources*.

Resistance and Compassion

Remember, your growth will be met by resistance from some of those around you, including family and friends. Moreover, there will be aspects within you that resist growth as well. Anyone that you encounter who is not on their own path of growth and transformation will likely experience your efforts to change as a threat to their desire for comfort and the status quo. Be compassionate with everyone!

Do not defend yourself or argue with anyone. Change will come to each person in their own time and way.

It is not your responsibility to change anyone except yourself.

Most importantly, as you begin to make changes and meet to-be-expected resistance, do not forsake your new direction. Stay true to your vision. The Camino is not over. You are *still walking*; you are on the Camino's second half.

A Dream

Another significant moment when an impactful nightly dream (inspiring, disturbing, or mysterious) may visit is after you arrive home.

Recall the dream with as much detail as you are able, especially feelings you remember having, and images you remember seeing in the dream. Record the dream, in writing or by voice recorder, using present tense.

Don't be concerned about interpreting the dream's meaning—allow the pulsing energy of the dream to move you. Notice where or what the dream's energy touches inside you. Where do you feel it in your body? What moment/place on your Camino holds energy that is similar to the energy in your dream? Give your dream a title. Play with the words and images. Dreams are full of puns, look for them.

For more on dream work, see the book, *A Little Course in Dreams*, by Robert Bosnak listed in *Resources*. His writing is non-technical, easily accessible, and with many practical suggestions.

Slowly Unpack

If at all able, leave your pack mostly as it is for a while. Perhaps remove and continue to wear some of your pilgrim clothes as a tactile visual reminder that you are metaphorically still walking the Camino.

Pilgrim clothes (their sight, feel and smell) are powerfully evocative of the experience you had while physically walking.

Not immediately unpacking and putting everything away is a physical and emotional help to homecoming.

In every way possible, prolong the sensory experience of your walk. It says to yourself and others, *I am still on the Camino.*

When the time does come to unpack and put things away, consider doing it with a trusted friend and/or your companion/mentor present. Share with them the stories that are awakened by the sight, feel, and smells of the items as you pull them from your pack.

VIII

LIVING INTO YOUR OWN STORY

How do we make the journey part of our lives once we are back in the daily grind? I see the time of return as reintegration time, a time to recall as much as possible about the trip. And again, storytelling allows things to `come up', and 'to trust your own wisdom.' We must remember: The journey is a miniature of the bigger one which is life.

Joan Marler
in *The Art of Pilgrimage*

The more (pilgrims) turn the riddle over in their mind, the more it will become involved with their own deepest instincts and desires.

Alexander Eliot
Earth, Air, Fire, and Water

Which moments gleamed brighter, gave you pause, challenged all your previous beliefs, reconfirmed your belief in a (higher) power? How did you happen upon them? Were they self-willed, the result of punctilious planning, or were they serendipitous? Did you feel any strange visitations of joy?

Epiphanies sometimes flash and flare for pilgrims, but there are also flickering moments of discovery on your journey, seen out of the corner of your eye. Can you recapture them now that you are home?

Phil Cousineau
The Art of Pilgrimage

Read the *Before You Walked* Letter

Within a week of returning home, read the letter you wrote yourself before you left for the Camino. Now that you have walked, how would you answer the questions you had before you left? Write a journal entry or voice record your response to that letter now that you have returned.

Most Important Element

The presence of a trusted and committed companion/mentor with whom you repeatedly share your story in detail is the most important element in helping you integrate your Camino experience and lessons learned.

See *Chapter II, Before You Leave* for guidelines on choosing someone to receive and deeply listen to your story. In the event that there is no one in your life appropriate to this role, please consider beginning to work with a professional counselor, mentor, skilled listener or even a therapist.

The more you repeat your Camino stories with your companion/mentor and trusted friends, the more the story becomes a part of the very fiber of your being. In a real way, the story of your Camino is one of your life's most important scriptures.

As you repeat your stories, the journey continues to deepen, the lessons become more clear and compelling and new layers of meaning come into view.

In sharing the details of your story, share your feelings about what you are describing in the story and the story's impact on your life. Ask your trusted friend to listen for how the telling of the story changes and deepens with every repetition.

Ask your companion/mentor to share with you anything they observe about you and the story, including how they experience your story evolving over time and how they perceive you evolving as well.

Brief Stories

The family and friends who feted you when you departed may be busy with their own lives and mysteriously disappear when you call to share your travel stories, (photos) and astonishments. Prepare yourself. It will be harder than you think to find an audience for your stories.

Phil Cousineau
The Art of Pilgrimage

Friends and family will primarily want entertaining stories, including descriptions of food, humorous or scary moments and colorful sights as well as accounts of places that astonished you. Many aren't interested in listening to an account of your personal growth and realizations about your life. They want to hear "highlights of the trip," so give them just that.

Don't be surprised if some of your friends try to diminish or dismiss your experience and/or turn the focus of the conversation to another topic or back on themselves.

Some people engage in this behavior to reduce their own anxiety. In light of your Camino experience, they may consciously or unconsciously feel inferior to you. To avoid their own pain, they might pull away from your story by using humorous asides, telling jokes or completely changing the subject.

Still others will feel so challenged by what you are sharing and by the growth you are experiencing that they will literally or metaphorically distance themselves from you in subtle or overt ways.

They do so because the growth and change they see in you reminds them of the growth and change they are probably avoiding in their own lives. Examining their own lives could be too painful and stress-inducing; and for whatever reason, it may not be the right time for their own journey.

—

The easier choice for them is to distance themselves from you, as you are the stressor. If you feel this "distancing" by any friend or family member, do not try to re-engage them with your story, or in any way believe you must fix them, enlighten them etc. Their journey of growth awaits them in their own way and time.

Sharing in-depth stories with people not equipped to hear them may prove frustrating and increase your sense of isolation. Also sharing intimate stories in settings that aren't conducive to real listening is fruitless.

If the person you are sharing with isn't connecting with you, you may easily feel you are being dismissed, not heard, not understood or not valued. This kind of frustration can weaken, injure or even end a friendship.

Indeed, some friendships that existed before walking may not be able to continue upon your homecoming. Should that be the case, know that these friendships had probably been "on the ropes" for a while before you left for the Camino.

Save the deeper dive for your companion/mentor who by mutual agreement is willing to listen to your stories without judgment or anxiety, as well as others who know the cost of change and growth in their own lives.

Read the *After You Walked* Letter

Forty to sixty days after arriving home, read the letter you wrote yourself as you ended your walk. Consider having your first reading be in the presence of your companion/mentor and reflect on the following thoughts:

What, if anything, you wrote surprises you now?

- Which pieces of the letter had you forgotten?
- Which parts of the letter do you agree with now, a few months later? Which parts do you disagree with? Which parts would you change?
- Are the life lessons you named still accurate or how have they changed/developed since returning home?
- What observations does your companion/mentor have upon hearing the letter?

Re-read both the "before you walked" and "after you walked" letters periodically (perhaps once a month) for the first year after your return. Note the changes in yourself that you observe. Ask your companion/mentor to note the changes she/he observes in you.

Listen in a Relaxed and Open Manner to Others

Your family members and friends' lives went on while you were away. As much as you wish to have them share in your stories, it is very important for you to make an intentional time to really listen to their stories, hopes, concerns, etc.

While you were away taking time to reflect, they were at home in the work-a-day world with the usual strains of routine, finances and time pressures. They need you to be present to them in an open and gracious way.

As you listen to them, refrain from mentioning the Camino. Demonstrate that as they share, you are fully present to them, rather than thinking about what you want to say next.

As you hear the details of their life, feel their feelings. Take in and reflect back to them their joys, hurts and concerns. Are you noticing a greater capacity within you to truly empathize with their lives?

Pruning and Waiting

One of the gifts you receive from your walk and repeated telling of the story is the ability to see what is really true in your life. Seeing what is, you are then able to prune away those things, activities and perhaps friendships that no longer serve you well.

As painful as the pruning is, whether it be friendships, material things or even your job, find solace in the fact that the pruning is a gift. If you retain whatever no longer serves you well, your spiritual, intellectual and emotional growth is stunted.

Life's journey is about growth, continual growth. Hanging on to that which does not support transformation drags us down and hinders further growth.

In the growing cycle, remember the value of fallow time, in gathering the needed nutrients for new growth.

The space created in your life as a result of pruning will probably not be immediately filled. Ultimately renewed passion, purpose and friendships will arrive.

Grieve what is passing away, let be, and wait patiently for the new.

IX

AIDING INTEGRATION

A man's work is nothing but this slow trek to rediscover, through the detours of art, those two or three great and simple images in whose presence his heart first opened.

Albert Camus

Throughout this book, I have shared the aphorism: pass by what you do not love. As true as this was during the time you walked, it is equally true for your homecoming.

You likely return with a honed sense of yourself, knowing yourself better than ever before, and knowing what works and does not work for you with far more clarity. Now, use this self-awareness as you integrate your Camino walk and lessons into everyday life.

As you read the ideas and suggestions that follow, listen for those that make the most sense to you. Focus on no more than two or three ideas at most. Then, commit yourself to doing them.

Treasured Item

Place a treasured item you acquired as part of your Camino journey where you will see it daily.

Over multiple Caminos, my treasured item is the Pilgrim Credencial that holds the sellos (stamps) I received from the places I visited and albergues or inns where I slept along the journey.

2012 Pilgrim Credencial

The credencial reminds me of the walk rather than any particular place or destination. Once a week I sit with my credencials. I take the time to remove them from their plastic sleeve, feel their texture, run my fingers over the crimpled paper, smell the musky aroma, and note their smudge marks, often the result of that day's rain. In so doing, I immerse myself again and again in my own story.

The weathered and worn appearance of my credencials reminds me of *kintsugi*, the Japanese practice of repairing old pottery cracks by infilling them with gold dust. In this way, the cracks strengthen the vase while making it all the more beautiful. To me, my credencials are a living organism. As I caress them, they seem to breathe, and I experience even more of my own stories.

Read

Reading (or re-reading) Camino accounts by other pilgrims after your own journey will help you recall forgotten memories. While other pilgrims' experiences may not have been the same as yours, the truths that they share will help you refine your own. As you read their stories, write down or make a voice recording of your own tales and memories as they surface.

Watch

A host of YouTube documentaries and movies about walking the Camino are now available. Watch a few or a lot. I recommend the ones listed in *Resources* at the back of this book. Watch them alone with your journal in hand, jotting notes and further reflections.

The sights and sounds of the Camino are particularly helpful in awakening your senses. Memories are not only stored in the brain, but also in cells throughout the body. Awakening your physical senses aids memory recall. Watching these documentaries and making notes or journal entries after your return will do the same for you.

Now is also an apt time to watch them together with trusted friend/s and maybe family as well.

Share

Share your experiences and Camino stories in as many ways as you can with fellow pilgrims. Forums, newsletters and pilgrim gatherings awaken your memories, stir your feelings and remind you of lessons you learned. Sharing your Camino experiences teaches you again by reminding you of the details of your own journey.

Nature

At least once a week spend a significant amount of time in nature. Do this for at least three months after your return and perhaps do it indefinitely.

Plan one day a week where your only mode of transportation is walking (or cycling or horseback if you cycled or rode a horse on the Camino). Remember, your whole body stores memories. Spending time in nature stimulates all your senses, awakening memories and releasing endorphins which provide a sense of well-being.

Cleanse

Cleanse and de-clutter your living space to more accurately reflect the new you and the changes you are trying to make. Clean and simplify your home and give away items that no longer serve you well.

If medically appropriate for you, consider doing a cleansing body fast and/or sacred sweat soon after your arrival back home, again 40–60 days later, and then again in the days before your Gathering and Celebration.

Create

Sort your Camino photos and/or videos and assemble a photo/video journal that tells the story and lessons of your Camino. Or create a collage from *your* Camino photos and mementos.

For more on collage making, helping to tell your soul story, see Seena B. Frost's book, *SoulCollage Evolving*, listed in *Resources*.

If you have been walking the Camino as an intentional rite of passage, consider creating a more permanent signifier of the inner changes you are making. One way might be designing a tattoo and inking your body, physically expressing your commitment to continual growth. Other signifiers used in classical rites are body piercing, scarification and/or a shaved head.

Acquire

Enshrine a treasured item you brought home from the Camino. Acquire a gem, stone, or piece of jewelry that signifies the change/s in your life.

If this treasured item is something you wear, develop the habit of putting on the emblem when you awaken and taking it off before you go to bed. If your treasured item is not something you wear, then develop a ritual that connects you daily to it.

How Do I Wish to Live?

At the Sanctuario of Santa Maria a Real in the village of O Cebreiro, the text of this *Pilgrim's Prayer* by Fray Dino hangs on the wall. It carries no date. The prayer's final stanza reads:

> *If from today*
> *I do not continue walking your path,*
> *searching and living according*
> *to what I have learned;*

if from today
I do not see in every person, friend or foe,
a companion on the Camino;

if from today
I cannot recognize [God,
the God of Jesus of Nazareth
as the one God of my life.]

I have arrived nowhere.

To read the entire text, Google *Pilgrim Prayer* by Fraydino.

If you wish, say the phrase I placed in brackets in the way that has meaning for you.

More importantly, as you reflect on the prayer, ask yourself:

How do I wish to live—
according to what I am learning?

What is the Camino trying to teach me
about myself and my world?

Something in your answer to these questions is likely a key to your integration.

Compose an Agreement

Reflecting on your Camino and your answer to the above questions, compose an agreement with yourself. As a way to touch all the needed bases in composing your agreement, here is a process called, *Circle of Change*:

Contemplation
> *Do I really want to do this, or not really?*

Motivation
> *What is to be gained from the changes?*

Preparation
> *What needs to be in place to support the changes?*

Implementation
> *Making the changes.*

Maintenance
> *What happens when I forget and slip back to my old ways? How do I remember and get back on track?*

In writing the agreement, describe the changes that you wish to make; detail the efforts that you will engage in to make them.

Set calendar dates to review the agreement and make any needed adaptations.

Consult with your companion/mentor as you prepare to write the agreement. Share your ideas, asking him or her to respond and dialogue with you about them.

Also ask your companion/mentor to hold you accountable, and help you pace yourself with the changes you seek to implement.

Finally, put the agreement in a visible place as a frequent reminder of your intention and commitment.

Do you have a meditation spot or personal altar where you would visually see your agreement at least once a day? Or if appropriate in your household, attach it to the refrigerator door.

X

CLOSURE
FIRE—GATHERING—SERVICE

...become the source that makes
the river flow, and then the sea
beyond. Live in this place
as you were meant to and then,
surprised by your abilities,
become the ancestor of it all,
the quiet, robust and blessed Saint
that your future happiness
will always remember.

David Whyte
poem, "Coleman's Bed"

Closure

Closure does not happen at any particular moment.
Closure is not taking part in a ritual fire or having a
celebratory gathering. True closure is a gradual process
whereby the Camino's lessons and gifts are brought
into daily life.

The first weeks and months after returning home, the
Camino is more in the foreground as you contemplate
what you have learned and how to make it part of your
on-going, ordinary day.

Alexander John Shaia

Mining the Camino's gold, will take at minimum the first hundred days post-return; and more often nine months to one year. This span of time is about keeping your focus on naming the Camino's lessons and beginning to put them into practice.

After this initial period, what comes next are visible actions (Fire Ritual, Celebratory Gathering, etc.) that signal to yourself and others that you are changing from a primary focus on the Camino and returning to everyday life with gift and responsibility.

As you now move into the rest of your life, consider periodically returning to the Camino's lesson. With your companion/mentor, re-assess the commitments you made, continue to be accountable for using your gifts and talents, and review how you are giving yourself in service to other pilgrims, and indeed, to life itself.

At least once a year—maybe the anniversary of the day you began walking, ended walking or arrived back home—make an in-depth review of your Camino experience.

Read your "before" and "after" letters, journal, agreement etc. Take time to again look at your photos. Be in touch with pilgrim friends and others you met as you walked. And spend time with your companion/mentor. Together, review your Camino experience and reflect on how you see its impact on your life now, even years later.

Ritual Fire and Burning

A fire ritual can be a powerful, vulnerable and intimate moment. It can serve as a ceremony of closure
for the more overt portion of your Camino, signaling
that you are now entering a lengthy, gradual and more
hidden time of integrating the Camino's lessons into
your everyday life.

Chapter V, Once Walking Has Ended, explains my ad-
vice to not give a lot of energy to a ritual fire at your
turn-around place. The reasoning is that most today are
using that fire to announce closure and the end of "the
Camino." Your turn-around place is not the Camino's
end. Rather, it is a needed pause before beginning the
second half of your Camino, the return home.

Consider a ritual fire between ninety days and nine
months after returning home. Where and when would
you like to do this? Who do you wish to join you?

At minimum, your companion/mentor needs to be
present. It is important that you be "witnessed" at
this fire and its burning.

Considering the importance of this moment, ponder if
the presence of your larger family and friends will be
a support or diminishment?

If their presence will serve as a support, you might
consider this ritual fire as part of your Gathering. The

section entitled, Gathering at Ninety Days to Nine Months, later in this chapter outlines suggested details for this.

Consider four different reasons for the fire and its burning:

- Gratitude
- Release
- Naming gifts and talents with which you have been blessed
- Stating your ongoing commitment to personal growth and transformation.

Gratitude

In whatever way you pray or meditate, give thanks for all the benevolence you have received along the way. This statement of gratitude has tremendous impact if it is done while the fire is being lit.

Is there a picture or image you wish to place near the fire—an image of Spirit, God, Higher Power to which you dedicate this fire? Be cautious not to place the images so close to the fire that they could burn or be singed.

When I engage this ritual, I place four images near the fire: a contemporary icon of St. James as a Celtic Pilgrim, a picture of the Black Madonna of Montserrat, the Quadratos logo/four-armed equidistant cross in a circle, and an image of the Cosmic Christ.

In whatever way you wish, name or call upon Spirit etc. to witness you and witness that which, through this fire, you choose to both release from your life and to claim as personal commitment as you move forward in your life.

Release

My story: I am not a fan of burning my pilgrim clothes. It seems like both a waste of money, as well as a potential loss of the sensory experience of the walk. Pilgrim clothes are treasures brought home. Simply putting on the clothes may powerfully evoke the experience of the Camino.

However, there may well be felt meaning in burning one item of clothing. The item I have chosen (over a series of fire rituals) is a pair of socks—socks worn almost daily on the Camino and that each night held the sweat of my own anxiety and physical pain.

Burning these socks served as a physical and emotional release—helping me to let go of the anxiety I held as I walked and hold still in my life back home.

During these fire rituals, I have also burned small strips of paper. On each strip is written a "negative thought," that I had become more aware of as I walked.

These negative thoughts often centered around not being good enough, such as:

Look at how quickly that person is walking. They are better than me. I need to push myself more.

I wish I had walked the Camino when I was younger and in better physical shape.

The walk is hard enough, do I really need to deny myself food, alcohol, headphones, music, etc.?

Additionally, I burn strips of paper on which I have written the names of individuals and situations that were part of my life in the past but now are holding me back from greater growth.

The release is always with gratitude for what has been, even as it is clear I need to move forward on a different path.

Gifts/Talents

> *The force that called you (to walk)*
> *is asking for something vital only you can give.*
> *What is it? What can you give back?*
>
> Phil Cousineau
> *The Art of Pilgrimage*

Each of you have been given unique talents and gifts. The Camino as a rite of passage will make you aware of these.

Over the first months after returning home, and in conversation with your trusted friend, you will hopefully become more aware of your talents, claim them and commit yourself to offering them in the world.

With this third burning, what particular object or saying would you like to burn—as an offering to Spirit and to the fire as a gift? This burning is a visible action, stating your acceptance of your gifts and talents and understanding that you are now obligated to share them with others.

Commitment

As you reflect on your gifts/talents and what you received from the Camino, write out your commitments. Write the same identical text on three pieces of fine paper or parchment.

One you will burn in the fire. The second is to be given to your trusted friend, who is charged with holding you accountable for these commitments. The third is for you to keep, placing it in a prominent place so it may be a frequent reminder of your commitments.

Sign and date each copy and ask your trusted friend

to also sign and date them. Your trusted friend serves as a witness to hold you accountable, as a confidant, a fellow human and a tangible expression of Spirit.

Gathering at Ninety Days to Nine Months

Have a gathering and celebration ninety days to nine months after you return home. As you arrive home, share with family and friends that there will be a celebration at least three months away. It is important to bring them into the process, letting them know that your "returning home" is not just a matter of walking through the door.

The work of returning takes a long time. Give yourself at minimum one month after returning before you even consider setting a date for this Gathering.

About forty days after returning, begin to make specific plans for your gathering. Make the tone of the gathering true to who you are (festive, somber, large, intimate, loud, quiet, etc.). Who would you like to be present? Are pilgrims you met or walked with to be invited? Determine the type of location (home, pub, park, wilderness?). What food/drink will you serve? Might it be a Spanish or usual pilgrim menu?

Most importantly, discuss with your companion/mentor, which Camino experiences and lessons you wish to share at the gathering, and how you would like to share them (i.e., photos, film, music, poetry, dance, spoken words, etc.).

Consider a memento or gift for each person you have invited to gather with you. What might be a simple yet meaningful gift? A line of poetry, a wise saying that captures a piece of your Camino lesson, an image or picture from the Camino, a scallop shell, etc.?

During the gathering, in a way that is right for you, offer an expression of gratitude for your family and friends, for their presence in your life, and for all you have learned from them and others along the way.

In your way and style, ask your friends and family to share with you all the growth they have seen in you. Finally, ask for their good wish (blessing) as you continue to integrate your Camino and its lessons.

Serving Others and The Camino

The Pilgrim's Law:
A soulful (pilgrim) replenishes the camp
for those who will follow,
by sharing whatever wisdom
the pilgrim's been blessed
with those who are about to set out
on their own journey.

Phil Cousineau
The Art of Pilgrimage
(inspired by Rene Daumal's *Mount Analogue*)

Alexander John Shaia

In gratitude for this experience and all you have learned, commit to serving those discerning or preparing for a Camino walk. From local pilgrim clubs to national organizations there is ample opportunity to share of your experience, counsel and learnings.

If you sense a deeper call, you might volunteer for two weeks to a month as a hospitalero (host) in an albergue or refugio (hostels where pilgrims may sleep).

Consider service to the Camino itself. One idea is to carry a few trash bags and disposable sanitary gloves with you when you go out for a walk. While walking, pick up any trash you see along the way. Moreover, make a personal commitment to not leave trash as you walk.

Another way of being in service to the Camino itself is to return to Spain, as some former pilgrims have done and volunteer to clean or repair sections of the path, restore damaged or missing signage, etc.

The Wisdom and The Power to Serve

Everyone has gifts and talents to share.

My belief is that personal fulfillment comes from sharing those gifts and talents. The ultimate task of a Camino is to know your gifts and to know that you must offer them freely to each and all.

What are your gifts and talents?

With what freedom and joy do you share them?

Campbell's words eloquently sum The Return:

> *The ultimate aim of the quest,*
> *if one is to return,*
> *must be neither release*
> *nor ecstasy for oneself,*
> *but the wisdom and the power*
> *to serve others.*

Joseph Campbell
Myths to Live By

XI

A CLASSIC RITE OF PASSAGE

This chapter is for those who would like to know more about classic rites of passage, their stages, sequence, and benefit. The information in this section is a synthesis from my forty-year study of Rites of Initiation, Ritual, Myth, Jungian Psychology, Mystical Christian Spirituality and years of leading individuals and communities through rites of passage.

For more information and to read the source material on rites of passage, see Resources *at the rear of this book and* www.quadratos.com.

What *is* a Classic Rite of Passage?

A classic rite of passage, initiation or transition is a four-stage process wherein an individual is tested by particular ordeals and trials under the tutelage of a mentor. A rite offers an individual or a community the possibility of learning what is needed in order to make a transition from one phase or station of life to another.

Being witnessed by at least one other person, if not one's family or community, is an essential part of a rite of passage. The witness provides a "holding" presence, and has a critical role that includes:

- witnessing your journey
- extending a neutral sense of care through the ordeals (neither cheerleading, nor disparaging)
- helping you name the gifts that may be awakened
- offering ways to increase your skill in using your gifts
- holding you accountable for using your wisdom and gifts in service and for the greater good.

Classic rites of passage contain ordeals, with an uncertain outcome. As a result, a true rite can be an intense, anxiety-provoking experience. When undergoing a rite, you often experience large emotion, anger or deep disappointment with a mentor, guide, outer authority or someone that you expect to *care about you* or *save you*.

Ordeals and uncertainty within a Camino walk are key elements that enable the experience to potentially be a rite of passage. Because of an uncertain outcome, classic rites allow you to observe yourself in stressful situations, and potentially learn about your personal thinking and feeling styles as you meet or avoid tests.

Ultimately, a rite of passage is an opportunity to practice living the inner seasons and rhythms that you are likely to experience for the rest of your life.

In this way, a classic rite of passage is your life in miniature, whereby you potentially receive knowledge of yourself, and have an opportunity to release wounds as well as build skills for the next phase of your life.

Classic rites of passage have universal, common elements. Whether conducted by indigenous peoples, great spiritual traditions or contemporary psychological methods, a classic rite contains seven elements:

- Presence of an ongoing mentor
- Includes a Four Stage Process:
  surrender, trials, boon/gift, return-service
- Surrender to an intense period of trial and testing.
- Possibility that you will *not* learn the needed lessons, thereby 'failing' to transition at that moment.
- Naming your gifts and accepting that you *must* share them with your community and others.
- Community's witness of you, and their acceptance of your changed status and cognitive/emotional/spiritual abilities.
- Lengthy time of honing your skill so that you may both offer your gifts and serve more effectively.

Alexander John Shaia

The Benefits of a Classic Rite

*It has often been said that one of the characteristics of
the modern world is the disappearance of any meaningful rites of initiation.*

*Of primary importance in traditional societies, in the
modern Western world significant initiation is practi-
cally nonexistent.*

*In philosophical terms, initiation is equivalent to a ba-
sic change in existential condition; the novice emerges
from his ordeal endowed with a totally different being
from that which he possessed before his initiation; he
has become another.*

Mircea Eliade
Rites and Symbols of Initiation

Having spent decades as a spiritual director, educator
and Jungian psychotherapist, I believe there is an inher-
ent human need for periodic change at a structural level,
which is what I mean by the word "transformation."

Such all encompassing change is a pulse within the
cells of our body and I believe throughout the Cosmos.
However, within us as humans, something attempts to
pull us back, retard movement, and hold us at a lower
level of development.

For human millennia, spiritual and cultural rites of passage have been a means used to support structural change and mitigate against that within which would hold us back from transformation. Pilgrimage has been a significant and ordinary means for both a spiritual and cultural rite of passage.

Under certain circumstances in modern life, individuals, families and communities need psychotherapy to help them make a structural change. However, as a general principle, rites of passage can ably serve most people as a means of growth and transformation.

A Rite is Communal

What are the benefits in participating in a rite of passage? A rite is not private nor solely about the individual. A rite is inherently communal. In earlier times, the visibility of a rite announced to the community that change was beginning, it had to be supported, and both the initiate/s as well as the community would be required to do the work of negotiating a changed relationship with each other.

The re-negotiating of the relationship reminds us that every rite of passage has a death-like aspect. An individual cannot undergo change without the community also letting go of what has been and embracing a new and unknown future.

A Rite Requires a Mentor

Many may believe that they can negotiate change on their own, saying "I can do this for myself." Yet, we in the West need to un-learn many falsehoods, including the lie that life should be comfortable, stable, and devoid of risk or suffering.

A mentor is someone who has passed through the stage we are entering, knows more than we do about the transition, and firmly—yet with respect—hold us accountable to complete the tasks of the passage. A mentor is essential. No one can self-initiate.

Transformation holds tumult. Our "I" is unaccustomed to the work of structural change and will unreflectively clamp on to what is known. Without a mentor, we easily fall prey to the siren call to remain numb, dim and locked in an imagined golden yesterday.

An effective mentor is our best safeguard against self-delusion, helping us not abandon the journey and learn to live with more authenticity.

A Rite Has a Map

The pattern within a rite of passage matches the sequence of growth and transformation described by psychological theory as well as ancient myths and great spiritual traditions. The pattern is neither arbitrary nor nonsensical. It is actually part of the genius found in the classic rites.

The structure of the classic rites teaches you the precise steps and stages of growth and transformation. By experiencing a classic rite, you come to know in your body the rhythm of transformation, enabling you to discern its flow in your life, and coming to trust it in the same way one trusts the cycle of nature's seasons.

Knowing that one of the classic rites of passage mimics the pattern of growth and transformation throughout all of life aids our ability to trust and have courage when we find ourselves severely tested and in chaos, surrounded by what seems to be free-floating anxiety.

Today, some people and organizations are taking up the effort to restore rites of passage in western culture. However, many of these newly created rites do not understand the four-fold structure and the integral significance of each part to the whole.

As a result, many of these *new* rites lack a mature expression of the third and fourth stages—discerning the gift, returning, negotiating with community and service. As a result, while they offer some benefit to an initiate, these rites cannot offer the depth of transformation held within the classic rites.

I use the term 'classic rites' in an effort to distinguish the fullness of the ancient rites from the partial nature in some of the new rites.

The classic rites hold an inestimable treasure. They are not empty gestures, punitive or sadistic trials or merely self-congratulatory moments. A classic rite of passage holds the deepest wisdom of life.

Classic rites provide us a core map for living, help us understand outmoded attitudes and patterns we experience when under stress, offer us the opportunity to skill-build more effective ways to respond to difficult circumstances, to know our unique gifts, and to be mentored in offering our gifts for the greater good.

Finally, the classic rites require a process of homecoming in which an initiate and her/his community are *obliged* to negotiate a new relationship with each other.

Throughout Your Life

A common misperception is that a rite of passage is only about the transition from childhood to adolescence or adolescence to adulthood. Hardly! Every significant life event—birth, adolescence, marriage, partnering, beginning and ending work, divorce, mid-life, elder hood, major illness and dying—can be a moment for a rite of passage.

Many of these life events are the reasons we go on pilgrimage in general and the Camino in particular. However, simply going or simply walking is not enough for the Camino to become a classic rite of passage. Additional preparation and intent are needed.

Making the Camino a Rite of Passage

Here is my checklist of seven actions needed to transform your Camino into a classic rite of passage:

1. **The Camino Knows**

    As you walk, you will hear the saying, "the Camino knows" or "the Camino provides." What is meant by this is a belief that on the Camino, little to nothing happens by mere coincidence or chance. There is a wisdom presence that guides each of us toward our own personal growth. Examine everything as having purpose and meaning.

    My personal belief is that on the Camino, we walk on hallowed ground, soaked with the prayer and sweat of millions of pilgrims before us. Some describe this soil as holding a lei (energy) line that encourages growth and transformation.

    In whatever way you may understand the Camino, St. James, Jesus, Mary, Spirit, the Black Madonna, a lei line, etc., take this path to be your wise mentor.

Leave aside the idea of coincidence. Take the perspective that the Camino is providing exactly what you need for your own growth and transformation.

2.   Ask a trusted someone to be your companion/mentor before you leave to walk.

3.   Ask someone to remember you daily in prayer and good thought while you are away

4.   As you prepare, walk and as you return, practice mindfulness and living in the "now."

   Repeatedly bring yourself away from the idea of a physical destination. Gently remind yourself that your destination is "here" and "now."

5.   Your ordinary life is the only place where the work of sustainable change can happen.

   Walking is the place of awakening. Where you stop walking is where the second half of the Camino begins.

   Remember you are not yet *home* when you walk through the door.

   After returning home, meet with your companion/mentor often—perhaps weekly to twice weekly—for the first three months, at a minimum.

6. **Tell and re-tell the story of your Camino.**

    Notice how the story deepens by your continued telling and reflection. Gradually name the gifts received, and the changes you are being called to make.

    Develop a written agreement with yourself and your mentor, naming the changes the Camino has called you to make.

7. **Plan a Gathering at ninety days to nine months after arriving home.**

    Ask your companion/mentor as well as close family and friends to gather with you.

    At this Gathering, share with them the appropriate details of your inner story, and ask them to speak to the growth they see in you.

    Discuss, and negotiate, as needed, a change in your relationship with them. Also listen to their requests of you and how your relationship with them may need to grow.

    Taking into account all that has been shared and discussed, name the growth and development you wish to continue to make in your life, and ask them for their support.

The words of Joseph Campbell:

> We have not even to risk the adventure alone
> for the heroes of all time have gone before us.
> The labyrinth is thoroughly known . . .
> we have only to follow the thread of the hero path.
>
> And where we had thought to find an abomination
> we shall find a God.
> And where we had thought to slay another
> we shall slay ourselves.
>
> Where we had thought to travel outwards we
> shall come to the center of our own existence.
> And where we had thought to be alone
> we shall be with all the world.

from The Hero with a Thousand Faces

¡Buen Camino!

THE STORY OF MY (RE) DISCOVERY

It was around 11 p.m., on 1 November 2000. From my long-ago studies with Joseph Campbell, I had puzzled a deeper truth in early Christianity's choice of precisely four gospel texts and their sequencing into a Three-Year Sunday Reading Cycle.

What lay behind those choices? Were they the result of a believed oral tradition? Winners in a protracted theological tussle? Or were the four clearly inspired?

On that cold, clear, starry night in Northern New Mexico, I was up late reading Robin Griffith-Jones' book about the authors of the Gospel, *The Four Witnesses*.

Suddenly, an answer arrived to my long held queries— an answer that satisfied both my critical mind and longing heart. I reached for a legal pad and furiously wrote in a first attempt to describe the contour of this new landscape.

What followed has been years of research, questioning, challenging the premise, traveling thousands of miles, addressing hundreds of communities, leading seminars with spiritual leaders, clergy and all of us, and writing, writing, refining and rewriting.

Today that insight is called by a formal name—*The Journey of Quadratos*. And the most complete exposition to date is found in my book *Heart and Mind: The Four-Gospel Journey for Radical Transformation, Second Edition.*

Campbell had shown me a pattern in the human journey that is universal, sequential, and cyclical. It is recognized by every major religious tradition, mythology, school of psychology and understanding of pilgrimage.

On that cold night, I perceived how that journey forms the very heart of the Christian story and practice, and is the core truth that undergirds the four gospels. I have named this *The Journey of Quadratos* and its Christian telling as *The Four-Gospel Journey.*

Within Christianity, Quadratos provides a deeper understanding of Jesus the Christ and a new foundation for affirming early Christianity's choice of four gospels and the ancient—now restored—gospel reading sequence for Sunday worship.

At its most universal, the pattern of Quadratos is found in our experience of the four seasons and their cycle.

The four progressive paths of Quadratos correspond to the four parts of pilgrimage, to the four great questions of the spiritual life, and to the four traditional Christian gospels (Matthew, Mark, John, and Luke).

Each gospel's question and practice is revealed within a particular landscape and its human experience.

First Path: How do we face change?
    Climbing the Great Mountain of Matthew.

Second Path: How do we move through suffering?
    Crossing Mark's Stormy Sea.

Third Path: How do we receive joy,
        and experience oneness?
    Resting in John's Glorious Garden.

Fourth Path: How do we mature in service?
    Walking Luke's Road of Riches.

On that clear cold starry night, an answer arrived that seems to hold great significance.

Perhaps, just perhaps, it is a door to a new paradigm within world spirituality, Christianity, pilgrimage, psychology, the arts and even science.

THE JOURNEY OF QUADRATOS
Northern Hemisphere

THIRD PATH
How do we receive joy
and experience union?

Receiving the Gift
Ecstatic, Calm,
Visionary

Spring – East
First Light to
Mid-Morning

SECOND PATH
How do we move
through suffering?

Enduring all Obstacles
Strained by Opposites,
Exhaustion, Doubt,
Loneliness

Winter – North
Late Evening to
First Light

FOURTH PATH
How do we mature in
service?

Serving Life/Community
Gratitude, Give One's
Gift, Integration of
Opposites, Speak Truth
with Love

Summer – South
Mid-Morning to
Fading Light

FIRST PATH
How do we face change?

Hearing the Summons
Shock, Refusal, Unease,
Anxiety, Betrayal

Autumn – West
Fading Light to
Late Evening

THE JOURNEY OF QUADRATOS
Southern Hemisphere

THIRD PATH
How do we receive joy
and experience union?

FOURTH PATH
How do we mature in
service?

Receiving the Gift
Ecstatic, Calm,
Visionary

Serving Life/Community
Gratitude, Give One's
Gift, Integration of
Opposites, Speak Truth
with Love

Spring – East
First Light to
Mid-Morning

Summer –North
Mid-Morning to
Fading Light

SECOND PATH
How do we move
through suffering?

FIRST PATH
How do we face change?

Enduring all Obstacles
Strained by Opposites,
Exhaustion, Doubt,
Loneliness

Hearing the Summons
Shock, Refusal, Unease,
Anxiety, Betrayal

Winter – South
Late Evening to
First Light

Autumn – West
Fading Light to
Late Evening

THE HERO AND HEROINE'S JOURNEY

Joseph Campbell

As a university student in 1973, I stumbled into a seminar with a passionate and erudite professor teaching an advanced seminar on *Sacred Scripture and Great Myth*, offered through the theology department.

That professor was Joseph Campbell, arguably the world's pre-eminent mythologist. His impact on my life and work has been enormous.

Campbell names the human quest as the Hero and Heroine's Journey. This quest he calls a "monomyth," and divides it into four stages, comprising seventeen steps:

I. Hearing the Summons

1. The Call to Journey/Quest

2. Refusing The Call

3. Gifts/Mentor & Magical Aid Arrive

4. Crossing the First Threshold

II. Enduring Tests and Obstacles

5. Belly of the Whale

6. Road of Tests

7. Meeting with a Helpful Figure—Counsel Given

8. Meeting with Tempter-Temptress

III. Receiving the Boon

9. Encounter with Ultimate Power

10. Apotheosis—Receiving Greater Understanding

11. Ultimate Boon—Receiving a Taste, Sighting of the Quest's Goal

IV.   **Returning to Community**

12. Refusing the Return

13. Magic Flight—Magical Help to Return

14. Rescue from Without—Outer Life Presents Trials

15. Crossing of The Return Threshold—Many Tests and Errors

16. Skill in Two Worlds—Inner and Outer

17. Freedom to Live in the Moment—Neither Anticipating the Future, Nor Regretting the Past

Joseph Campbell
from *The Hero with a Thousand Faces*

RESOURCES

All are available as eBooks except where otherwise noted.

Power of Storytelling

Joseph Campbell, *Myths to Live By*, Stillpoint Digital Press, Joseph Campbell Foundation.

_____ with Phil Cousineau, *The Hero's Journey: Joseph Campbell on His Life and Work*, New World Library.

Jonah Sachs, *Winning the Story Wars*, Harvard Business Review Press.

Meditative Reading

Thich Nhat Hanh, *Fear: Essential Wisdom for Getting Through the Storm*, HarperOne.

_____, *How to Love*, Parallax Press.

_____, *How to Walk*, Parallax Press.

Henri J. M. Nouwen, *The Inner Voice of Love, A Journey Through Anguish to Freedom*, Doubleday.

David Whyte, *River Flow*, Many Rivers Press (book of collected poems).

Spiritual Practice

Jack Kornfield, *After the Ecstasy, The Laundry: How the Heart Grows Wise on the Spiritual Path*, Bantam. Audible, audio edition.

_____, *A Path with Heart: A Guide Through the Perils and Promises of Spiritual Life*, Bantam.

Matt Licata, *The Path is Everywhere, Uncovering the Jewels Hidden Within You*. Wandering Yogi Press. High recommendation—the chapter on the union of light and dark.

Seena B. Frost, *Soulcollage Evolving: An Intuitive Collage Process for Self-Discovery and Community*, Hanford Mead Publishers, Inc. *No eBook edition.*

Richard Rohr, *Everything Belongs: The Gift of Contemplative Prayer.* The Crossroad Publishing Company.

Pilgrimage/Camino

Phil Cousineau, *The Art of Pilgrimage,* Conari Press.

Nancy Louise Frey, *Pilgrim Stories: On and Off the Road to Santiago,* University of California Press.

China Galland, *Longing for Darkness: Tara and the Black Madonna,* Penguin books, 2007 *No eBook edition.*

Gina Marie Mammano, *Camino Divina, Walking the Divine Way,* Skylight Paths Publishing.

David Whyte, *Pilgrim,* Many Rivers Press (poems about pilgrimage and the Camino).

Sarah York, *Pilgrim Heart: The Inner Journey Home,* Jossey-Bass. *No eBook edition.*

Dreams

Robert Bosnak, *A Little Course in Dreams,* Penguin Random House.

Rites of Initiation

These are the classic anthropology texts on rites of passage.

Arnold van Gennep, *Rites of Passage*, University of Chicago Press.

Mircea Eliade, *Rites and Symbols of Initiation, The Mysteries of Birth and Rebirth*, Spring Publications, 1964, Kindle edition 2012.

Victor Turner, *The Ritual Process: Structure and Anti-Structure*. (Rites of Passage: Separation, Liminality, Reincorporation), Routledge, UK. *No eBook edition.*

_____, *From Ritual to Theatre: The Human Seriousness of Play. *No eBook edition.*

Mythic Journeys

Joseph Campbell, *The Hero with a Thousand Faces*, 1949. *No eBook edition.*

Joseph Campbell with Bill Moyers, *The Power of Myth, 1988. *No eBook edition. Book is based on the Public Broadcast Stations (USA) interviews of the same name.*

Clarissa Pinkola Estes, *Women Who Run with the Wolves: Myths and Stories of The Wild Woman Archetype*, River Wolf Press.

Maureen Murdock, *The Heroine's Journey: Woman's Quest for Wholeness*, Shambhala, 2013.

Richard Rohr, *Adam's Return: The Five Promises of Male Initiation*, Audible Audio Edition. The first half of this book is an excellent description of an initiatory process regardless of gender.

Alexander John Shaia with Michelle L. Gaugy, *Heart and Mind: The Four-Gospel Journey for Radical Transformation, Second Edition.* Amazon Paperback and Kindle, 2017.

Betty DeShong Meador, *Uncursing the Dark: Treasures from the Underworld, The Myth of Inanna*, Chiron Publications. *No eBook edition.* High recommendation—an in-depth look at a woman's rite of passage seen through the oldest known written western myth, from Sumaria, 5,000 BCE.

Paul G. Zolbrod, *Dine Bahane, Navajo Creation Myth*, University of New Mexico Press. *No eBook edition.*

Films/Documentaries

Walking the Camino: Six Ways to Santiago, Lydia B. Smith producer/director, 2014. www.caminodocumentary.org

> *An inspiring and visually stunning documentary, telling of six pilgrims' journey to Santiago. Of all Camino films, this one best captures its soul, inner experience and the likely individuals that one meets along the way.*

The Way, with Mark Shea, OverlanderTV.com, or YouTube, 2008.

> *Mid 30s Australian walks the Camino Frances, making a video-journal as he walks. Mark's reflections cut deeper than most. A close look will reveal the four paths of Quadratos in his pilgrimage.*

Cast Away, Robert Zemeckis, director-producer, with Tom Hanks and Helen Hunt, 2000.

> *Story of the sole survivor of a plane crash, marooned on an island for years, eventually rescued, and the adjustments he faces upon returning home.*

Remarkable storytelling, including the gift and challenges in returning home from a transformative experience.

Pilgrimage: The Way to Santiago, BBC Documentary, 2018.

Three episodes, each one hour, following seven well-known British individuals as they become pilgrims and walk the Camino Frances from St. Jean Pied de Port to Santiago, then to Finisterre.

Powerful dialogue, true to the feelings, thoughts and conversations found on the Camino. The aerial cinematography is breathtaking.

Retreats

Consider resting awhile once you have reached your turn-around place.

Many simple, quiet places exist near the coast in Galicia where you may spend a series of days. Here are two that I know and recommend.

Bela Muxia Albergue & Hostal
in Muxia
www.belamuxia.com

The Little Fox House
in the small village of Morpeguite
www.thelittlefoxhouse.com

Here are two contemplative places along the Camino Frances:

Flores Del Camino Retreat
in the picturesque village of Castrillo de los Polvazares
8 km west of Astorga
www.floresdelcamino.com

The Stone Boat
in Rabanal del Camino
www.thestoneboat.com

NOTES:

Since 2012, I have worn this cap every day I walk the Camino.

ABOUT ALEXANDER JOHN

Alexander John Shaia is a thoughtful and poetic man, living the ancient rhythms of his Lebanese and Aramaic heritage. As an author, educator, cultural anthropologist, spiritual director, and Jungian-Sandplay therapist, he is known as a creative, multi-disciplined thinker and passionate professional speaker.

With conviction, he invites us into spiritual practices for the twenty-first century—ones that cross traditional boundaries, encourage vital thinking and inhabit a genuine community of the heart.

He travels internationally, lecturing on The Journey of Quadratos and leading seminars and retreats. Each year, Alexander John guides an intimate band of pilgrims for up to 60 days on the Camino Frances as an intentional rite of passage.

When not on the road, he lives in the mountainous high desert of Santa Fe, New Mexico, and an old fishing village on the wild Galician coast. A perfect day finds him with his dog, a book of poetry, and in the presence of ancient trees.

PLEASE CONNECT

Sister and Brother Pilgrims,

I would love to hear from you. What has been your experience of returning home?

Let me know how I may improve this book or better serve your returning home.

And join the discussion on my Facebook page:

@Alexander John Shaia—Author & Journey of Quadratos

See www.Quadratos.com for more about my work and offerings, including the Camino I lead each year, as well as many podcasts and other interviews.

In the Quadratos store, you will find postcards and posters made from the image on the cover of this book. Also, we have orange wristbands with white writing that reads, 'Returning From Camino. Wisdom & Power to Serve.' These bands are excellent memory devices to help us remember to remember.

Ultreia y Suseia,
Alexander John

ACKNOWLEDGMENTS

First and foremost, there is deep gratitude for the presence and companionship of my 2012 Camino Family:

Amy Deibert	Joshua Barretto
Anne and Cliff	Marc Stolwijk
MacKinnon Munns	Michael (physician)
Doug and Jill Spaner	Nina Chong
Filippo Donadel	Philip (my nemesis)
Lisa Mennell	Reinhard Kogler
John Maier	Robin Brodsky
Jonathan Gaunt	

And a deep bow to every pilgrim I have walked with as well as those I have mentored—past, present and future. You are my great teachers.

Each time I walk the Camino, I am humbled by a legion of friends who patiently aid, gently encourage, and become the opportunity for me to learn my life lessons. There is not enough space for me to describe what each of you has offered me. In honor and gratitude, I place your names here on this wall as they are a radiant presence in my heart.

Adam Narloch	Anna Elizabeth Pitt
Alicia Kay Hoffman	Anne Ritchings & Kay Hankinson
Amanda & Tom Hedger	

Andrea Horner

Andrea & Luke Lingle

Anja Saunders

Angel & Celia of Bela Muxia

Anthony & Victoria Bolus

Benjamin Postma

Beth Bush-Donovan

Bethley Sullivan

Carey Franklin

Carmen C. Teirado-Fortier

Carol Kindchi & Lawrence Greenburg

Caroline & Stephen Leys

Caroline Issacs & Randy Mayers

Cath Connelly

Charles Tegner

Christophe Rouzé

Christy Blandford

Christy Sweeny

Colleen Ford-Dunker

Connie Cox

Darrell Smith & All the Staff of Alamo Heights United Methodist Church

Dave & Christina Pilkington

Dave Cutherell & Vicki Walsh

David Littleton

Deceased Members of the Shaia, Elkourie, Bolus, Massar, & Butrus families

Diana Garcia

Diane Whalen

Dora Bolus

Eden Elizabeth Nicholls

Elizabeth Albiston

Eva Maria Sanchez

Geraldine & J. Michael Gospe

Gertrud Nelson

Gina Vander Kam

Glenda R. Elliott

Glenn Gaunt

Glenn Siepert

Helen Summers

India Watkins

James Prescott

Jan Lustig & Nomi Green

Jane Hall

Janet & Andy Simmonds

Jean & Alan Henderson

Jean Holsten

Jeanette M Norris

Jennie & Julian Kenny

Jenny & Henry Burger

Jeremy Graeme Ball

Jessica Ryan

JL & Sharon Shaia

Jill K. Mabry

Joan Hanrahan

John Bulten & Morgan Attema

John Shaia & Lori Kim

Luke Alexander &
Adeline Kim

John & Sandi Steward

John Stuart

John Williamson

Jonathan & Pamela
Gaunt

Josie Abbenante

Judy Hall

Juliet Calabi

Kareme Shaia

Karin Delgadillo

Kathleen Bellefeuille-Rice

Kelly Tanis

Ken, Fonda & Zany
Shaia

Kenneth Kovacs

Kimberly Boone

Lavonne Williamson

Leslie Gilmour

Liz Elizabeth Helmore &
Nativa Travel

Lucia & Imanol of Hotel
Uson

Lydia B. Smith

Marc Heffner & Camino
Estrella

Maggie & John
Monroe-Cassel

Marcel Legendre

Marjorie Hoyer-Smith

Mark Shea

Martha Ann & Herbert
Bolus

Martha Iwaski

Mary & Ken Horst

Mary & Tom Williams

Mary Conner

Mary Ryllis-Clark

Matt & Renee Shumate

Megan & Joe
Stewart-Sicking

Mercedes & Maximo of
Molino Galochas

Michelle L. Gaugy

Michiel Crawford

Mike & Jasmine Morrell

Missional Wisdom
Foundation

Nicole Reinecker of Neek
Design

Nohealani & Walt
Stewart

Norman & Lisa Bolus

Pam Schwanke

Pamela Burnham

Paul & Theresa Bolus

Paula Pointer

Peggy Dunn Davis

Pete Holmes

Rachel Gaunt

Richard Hipps & Trinity
Baptist Church

Rob & Kristen Bell

Robin Neher

Sandra Lommasson

Sarah Louise Ricketts

Selema Butrus-Rookis

Seth Price

Sus & Puri of Casa de
Lema

Susan Dickson

Sylvie Eyral & Janis
Crays

Tracy Saunders of Little
Fox House

Vera & Bill Roughton

Veronica Cukro

Wesley M. Matlcok

William & Mary Faye
Shaia

To anyone whose efforts I have forgotten, my sincere
apology.

To two who work while I am on the road. You make
this all possible.

Donna Nicolson

Jan Lustig

To those who so graciously shared their heart and home
with me as I wrote and wrote:

Ellen Termine & Michael
Regets

Jennie & Julian Kenny

Linda & Bob Shumate

Pamela & Jonathan
Gaunt

Marie Morgan &
Berkeley Merchant

Nora & Timothy   Mary Wright
Speakman

To my editors, who are my teachers. This work has come to fruition because of your skill, perseverance, patience, and incredible kindness. Always, you have been kind.

Lynda Helmer   Ignacio Garrido
                        Manrique
Pamela Gaunt
                        Patrick Maiwald
Nora Speakman
                        Joy Jaber
Ellen Termine
                        Jose Luis Alonso

To Each and To All
My love and gratitude.

Alexander John Shaia

NOTES:

NOTES:

Alexander John Shaia

NOTES:

NOTES: